Y0-BXL-244

Encyclopedia of
Victorian Colored Pattern Glass

Book II
OPALESCENT GLASS from A to Z

by william heacock

Photography by Richardson Printing Corp.
Marietta, Ohio 45750

OTHER BOOKS BY WILLIAM HEACOCK

ENCYCLOPEDIA OF VICTORIAN COLORED PATTERN GLASS
Book 1 — Toothpick Holders from A to Z 9.95
Book 3 — Syrups, Sugar Shakers & Cruets 12.95
Book 4 — Custard Glass from A to Z 12.95
VICTORIAN COLORED GLASS PATTERNS & PRICES (an abridged
    version of Books 1, 2 & 3 in a handy pocket size) 8.95

FOR THE GAMBLES
With Everlasting Gratitude

TABLE OF CONTENTS

FOREWORD

This is a revised second edition of Book 2 of a series offering updated information for identification of Victorian colored glass. This volume concentrates on those patterns and novelties made in the popular opalescent ware which was massively produced from 1885 to circa 1910 in America.

A considerable number of changes, corrections and additions have been made to this edition, in order to keep my readers informed of the latest research findings. However, I cannot stress strongly enough that serious glass collectors not limit themselves to a single volume of this series. As new volumes are added, the latest update of information is offered pertaining to previous volumes. Each year brings new and exciting discoveries which unfortunately affects much of the data presented here. This author is doing everything possible to keep this series as factual and error-free as is humanly possible.

Due to increased printing costs, the Hobbs Glass catalogue referred to occasionally in the text is not being offered in this or any later edition. However, photostatic copies will remain available to serious glass collectors by sending $2 to the publisher.

HOW TO USE THIS BOOK

The book is divided into seven basic categories, listed in the table of contents on page 4. The first section will likely be overlooked by most people who buy this book, but it does contain many valuable bits of data for collectors, and I recommend that you read it.

Section 2 covers the pressed opalescent glass, those patterns which were part of a table service. This section, as well as all the others, are divided into text and illustrations. The pieces illustrated are numbered from 1 to 629, and are clearly labeled with their pattern names. The information pertinent to each pattern can be found in the text, which is alphabetically listed. The text offers figure numbers where illustrations are located.

Other chapters cover blown opalescent pattern glass, opalescent novelties, English glass, reproductions, last minute additions, old ad and catalogue reprints, and even a listing of corrections to the text of Book 1.

The illustrations on the title page are alphabetically categorized.

A LETTER TO MY READERS

I hope you can realize that bringing this book to press was one of the toughest things I have ever had to do. I wanted to make it as complete, as factual, as entertaining, and as easy-to-read as was humanly possible, without making the cost prohibitive for the average pocketbook. And yet I have not been entirely successful at any of them.

I realize now how futile my goals were. As far as a "complete" book, 650 pieces illustrated is an impressive qualification, and yet as I write this, I am tracing down leads on dozens of other unlisted items which are not named in this book. I am planning a sequel to Book 1 ("Toothpick Holders from A to Z"), and as Book 2 goes to press, already I see the need for a follow-up volume. So be patient. If your favorite piece is not in Book 1 or Book 2—perhaps it will be listed later.

As for factuality, it is apparent that I have undertaken a considerable amount of research to compile all this data in one place. Much of what you will read here has never been offered before. Very little is in repetition of Mrs. Hartung's earlier publication on this subject. Yet you cannot possibly hope to understand the futility in trying to trace down the origins of a piece of hand-blown glass which was never offered through advertisements, never trademarked, never shown in a catalogue that we know of. So 25 years from now, when some of these long-lost catalogues surface, and much of my data may be proved inaccurate, then I will stand corrected. I anxiously await that day. But until then, at least someone has stuck his neck out and made a decent educated guess.

Entertaining? I certainly hope so. The thousands of miles, the thousands of hours spent in preparations and production hopefully make this a book that will be fun to "flip" through for many years to come. Many of the items in this book are so rare that even the affluent collectors have little hope of owning them. But now they can at least enjoy the true color and beauty of many of these unattainable pieces.

As for "easy-to-read", I am afraid that is where you may feel I have failed dismally. I have prepared the text of this book as simply as possible, which also made it possible for me to disguise my inadequacies as a writer. The pattern information is presented in alphabetical order. However, the color plates were not arranged in alphabetical order (a feature so well liked about Book 1).

The primary reason for this was that most of the items illustrated in this book were loaned from a number of devoted glass collectors from all over this country, and were photographed over an extended period of six months. It would have been impossible to gather up all of these pieces for a single marathon photo session. Oh yes, I could have had all these lovely plates cut up and arranged alphabetically, but then these different collections would have lost their appeal as groupings from the various collectors. Certainly you must agree that there is nothing more impressive than a full page of cranberry opalescent, or an appealing display of water pitchers or syrup jugs. And who would have thought that the lowly-regarded white opalescent pieces would look as lovely as they do on page 84? Cutting up these color plates and re-arranging them alphabetically would have diminished their appeal.

Also, a considerable amount of scale would have been lost, because a closeup of a toothpick next to a longshot of a punch bowl would have dwarfed the impressive size of the larger piece.

I am well aware that the ensuing page-flipping will sometimes be frustrating when tracing down a certain piece of a certain pattern. I apologize to you, my readers, for this slight inconvenience in text arrangement, and hope you can see that the present form was the only answer.

ACKNOWLEDGEMENTS — "A Special Thank You from the Author"

How do you really thank someone? I owe so many people so much for their completely unselfish help in this project. Some made only a small contribution—others provided priceless help. But to all of them I owe a debt of gratitude which I will never forget.

So much has happened to me since the publication of Book I. By far, the most important thing is that through that first effort, I have met and become good friends with scores of people who share my enthusiasm over this series. All have offered unlimited use of their collections for future volumes in this series, and they will never know how honored I am by their unfailing trust.

Book II is indeed a group effort. No less than forty collectors and dealers from all over the country will be seeing their pieces pictured within the covers of this book. It is very hard to ask for help which requires personal sacrifice, but in virtually every case, these people offered to loan their prized possessions without even having to be asked. And in every case, their glass was returned exactly as it was loaned. Their trust in me has done wonders for my self-respect, and I am richer for the experience of having known them.

Two particular individuals, whose collections comprise more than 40% of this book, asked not to be mentioned in my book. I bow to their wishes, but I won't let their contribution to this volume go unnoticed. They have unselfishly shared their collection with thousands of other glass-lovers, and we all owe them something for that. These two people, from different parts of the country, started collecting opalescent glass when it wasn't as highly regarded as it is today, and I am happy for them both that they can be a part of a publication which will bring their collections even more regard. I cherish their friendship, and can never truly thank them enough.

A tremendous share of credit must go to Mr. Joe B. Bell, whose devotion to this project has been unequalled. He unselfishly packaged and mailed more than 20 boxes of glassware from his collection, claiming that the risks of mailing were small compared to the importance of the final project. When everything looked futile to me, a letter from Joe would arrive, bringing a whole new wave of enthusiasm. Joe shared every bit of information with me, no matter how trivial it may have seemed to him. This often resulted in an important discovery when pieced together with my own research findings. I have never had the privilege of meeting Joe, but when I do, I look forward to personally thanking him for his priceless contribution to the book. His name really should accompany mine on the by-line.

One hot day in June, 1975 I made a pre-arranged trip through Ohio, picking up glassware from collectors on my way to Marietta for yet another of the seemingly endless photography sessions. The day literally swept by, and will remain in my memory as long as I live. The first stop was at Bob & Jean Brocke's, collectors of blue opalescent. I walked out of their home with a considerable chunk out of their collection, but they never once showed any hesitancy. Further on, I stopped at the home of Tom and Betty Laney, who encouraged me to take whatever I needed from their collection. I walked out with three full boxes—mostly extreme rarities, which was all I needed at that time—and they never once pleaded for the safe-handling of their glass. Another two hours down the road to the Wendell Graves residence. Mrs. Graves, her sister-in-law Geraldine Gerson, and their families were all there to meet me, and they insisted that I stay for dinner. I spent three precious hours with this delightful family, and a box-full of glass was removed trustingly from their home. To all of you I extend the sincerest of thank you's. I want my readers to witness what lovely, fine and unselfish people you are.

From Indiana, Jack & Julie Mavis were the very first people to offer their collection for this project. Most of the items shown on the cover and practically all of the syrups and sugar shakers were borrowed from them. They are very good friends of mine, and it is a continual delight to be in their company.

Other Hoosiers who offered their assistance in this book include the Perry family (Lawrence, Mary Jane, and 2 of their 8 children, Kathy and Jane). The Perry's also had a hand in Book 1. One of the Perry boys, Al, was the photographer. I also want to thank Norman Russell, who with his late wife Dorothy, amassed an exciting collection of Albany glass over the years. I am certain Mrs. Russell would have been proud to know that her pieces are in this book, and I am grateful to Norman for his unselfish trust in me. A final Indiana thank you to Mr. & Mrs. Howard Elliott (you'll be seeing the majority of their collection in a later volume), Garr and Elsie Kitt, and my friend "Tiny" from Kokomo.

From Michigan, I want to thank Mr. & Mrs. La Verne Sweet, the Robert Hefners, Ms. Dayna Alexander, the Goldsberry's, and the staff and personnel at one of Michigan's finest antique shops, "The Sign of the Peacock."

From nearby Ohio, considerable credit goes to my dearest friends Ted and Ruth Heischmann, Judge Wilbur Armstrong and his adorable wife, Martha, Mr. & Mrs. Jay Bollinger, Mr. & Mrs. Al Berry, Loren Yeakley, Penny Sulley, and a big thank you to the well-known Cambridge glass experts, Lyle, Mary and Lynn Welker.

It is impossible for me to pinpoint each individual's contribution to making this book more complete, but rest assured it was substantial. Others who cannot go unmentioned are Ruby Fink, Jack Burk, Mr. & Mrs. Edd Sawicki, Mr. & Mrs. Gary Ellis, Robert & Pat Costa, Jennie Shultz, Jim Broom, Don Farrell Sr., Elmer Sharpe, and my dear dear friends from down Georgia way, Ed and Kathy Wait. I appreciate the trust you all had in me, and the individual sacrifices that you all made to help make the book a memorable one.

A word of praise for the fantastic work done by the photographer, Dale Brown. His insistence on perfection was sometimes nerve-wracking, but it is obvious that he knew what he was doing from the outstanding results you hold in your hands. I thank him for these high standards which made my book a thing of real beauty.

An equally high word of praise for the friendly management and staff of Richardson Printing Corporation, who always made me feel at home as I roamed among them admiring the work they were doing on this book.

A final thank you to the staff of the Oglebay Institute of Wheeling, W. Va., and its director John A. Artzberger. They granted the permission to reprint some of the pages from the Hobbs Glass Company catalogue, and allowed me to study the Jefferson & Beaumont Catalogues. I highly recommend this fine museum to any lover of American glass. It is a sheer delight to witness the outstanding collections on display there.

A TRIBUTE TO AN EARLIER PUBLICATION

In almost every case where two books are written on the same subject, one of two things occurs. Either the author of the second book completely ignores the existence of the first, or the author makes sly references and implications about erroneous information in the earlier publication.

In my own case, it would be awkward for me to present this book as though Mrs. Hartung's book did not exist. Too many pieces in this book carry pattern names which she provided, and I always believe in crediting the sources from which I acquired pattern names. My book will pick up where hers left off. There will be some conflict in our opinions and conclusions, and there will be some repetition, but I have tried to present this information in a way where it would appear fresh and interesting.

In some cases, I will be correcting incorrect information from her earlier publication, and I am sure she can understand the necessity for this. But I undertake this with humility and with reverence for the priceless work she has done in the field of glass research.

Rest assured that I am not representing myself as being any more knowledgeable than Mrs. Hartung—or any other author on early glass. However, when new research turns up answers to questions which were overlooked or incorrectly answered by previous researchers, I consider it my duty to report these conclusions no matter how discrediting it may appear.

The whole purpose of research is to discover the truth and report it as completely and factually as possible. To short-change our readers by presenting inaccurate data is a misjustice of the highest proportions. Thus, I have undergone considerable effort to avoid errors in this Book 2. I have also listed on page 103 a number of corrections and additions to the text of Book 1. As soon as this first volume goes into a second edition, these corrections will be made accordingly to the text.

No book can possibly hope to be completely void of mistakes. The opalescent glass field is so all-encompassing that there will undoubtedly be a number of items missing from the listings of pieces made. As these items are seen by me or properly reported to me, I will include them in a future edition of this Book 2.

A PICTURE IS WORTH A THOUSAND WORDS

It is immediately apparent that a great deal of expense was undertaken to present the illustrations in this book. This series will be the first serious study of the long-neglected field of Victorian Colored Pattern Glass, and it stands to reason there is only one way to present it. Not with long wordy descriptions of the patterns, but with detailed closeup photographs in lovely true color. Thus, this not only becomes a study of the different patterns and their makers, but also a testament to the variety of colors and decorations which were common to tableware from 70 to 90 years ago.

Pictured in this book are not only a representative example of a pattern, which is the common practice in most volumes (and understandably so), but in some cases several examples of a pattern are illustrated. I wanted this book to be as complete a reference as possible, naturally. To some this may seem a bit exorbitant. However, I feel it serves a definite purpose.

As the value of colored pattern glass increases, then each purchase becomes more and more of an "investment." Certainly, with a considerable amount of devotion and effort, there are a few "sleepers" and a number of "bargains" to be found, and your investment will have an even larger return in the long run. But as more and more people become knowledgeable, as the numbers of collectors increase, and as our cherished glass gets harder and harder to find at bargain prices, we will have to resign ourselves to "pay the price."

Thus, this book becomes one of the best investments you can ever hope to make. Is this the original stopper to this cruet? Is this a reproduction? Is this the correct base to this butter dish? Has this been ground down or polished? A quick check through the pages of this book will bring answers to these important questions *before* these ever-increasing investments occur, thus providing you with some small protections. Had I limited the pieces of the pattern shown to just a creamer or a butter, your protection against fraud would be considerably lessened.

All too often quality antiques are appearing on the market repaired, polished, and with mismatched parts. I hope that this book, with over 600 different examples illustrated, will help you in making better and safer investments.

ALL THAT IS WRITTEN IS NOT NECESSARILY TRUTH

I hope the day never comes when I feel that I have learned everything and that there is no more need for further research. And I hope I never reach the point where I cannot admit a mistake, because no one is more aware of my imperfections than I. I am relatively new on this scene, and many of the "old-timers" (for want of a better word) have a little trouble accepting the word of a young "whipper-snapper."

Listed on page 103 of this Book 2 are a number of corrections and additions to the text of my first book. Most of the "mistakes" were caused through no one's fault but my own. Had I purchased a copy of the recently published complete study of McKee glass, I would not have incorrectly attributed *Spearpoint Band* and *Sunk Honeycomb*. The "additions" were discovered through my own continuing research in this field or through the letters from devoted readers, supplying me with much-needed bits of data. To all of you who have written, my sincerest thanks.

As this book prepares to go to press, plans are being made for the second edition of Book 1 of this series. All too often, as new discoveries in this field are reported and documented, earlier publications continue to appear on the market in their original printed text, mistakes and all. To this author, this is a gross misjustice to present and future generations of glass collectors. Because of this practice, hundreds of new collectors are investing their hard-earned money under misguided pretenses.

The market for books on antique glass is somewhat limited, and most never make it into a second printing, let alone a second edition. But there are several which have become "standards" which continue to be reprinted over and over again. When later documented research proves many of their earlier reports to be incorrect, then it is sad to see this useless, out-of-date data sold to an unsuspecting public. I am **not** saying I do not want to see the fine works of the pioneers sold any more. I am saying that they should be updated. Literally thousands of facts have surfaced since publication of these priceless early works.

Glass documentation is still in its early stages. Were it not for my plans on continually updating each printing, then even my books would be relics of limited use in about 20 years. As the years pass new discoveries will be made, early catalogues will come to surface and be printed for **all** to enjoy and study, and information presented by me can be proved wrong. I look forward to this day, because I have such a serious interest in glass research, that knowing the truth is far more important to me than any discredit these new discoveries may bring my own works.

THE TRIALS AND TRIBULATIONS OF NAMING UNLISTED PATTERNS

This book contains dozens of patterns and novelties which have never before been listed. Following the precedent set by other glass authors, I have named those unlisted items for easy reference for collectors. This practice is not as simple as it sounds.

The extreme similarity in names of patterns has caused considerable confusion for many years. There must be literally scores of patterns which include the words "Loop," "Fine-cut," "Honeycomb," "Thumbprint," "Sunburst," "Fan," "Block" and the much over-used "Diamond." Get one word wrong or out of context and you have another pattern.

Due to the rising popularity of mail order sales in antiques, it becomes absolutely essential that any newly uncovered patterns have names assigned to them that will create as little confusion as possible. Certain researchers have even gone as far as naming patterns identically to others already named. How many Maple Leaf patterns will we have to bear? And there seems to be one too many *Regal* patterns. It has gotten to the point that the name of the pattern has to be preceded with the name of the company or with the words "opalescent" or "late."

I have often thought how useless it is to name a pattern according to its design. Some of the loveliest pattern names have nothing whatsoever to do with their design. A quick check reveals that in almost every case, these turn out to be the original manufacturer's name. If this practice of calling their patterns *Louis XV, Doric, Excelsior, Czarina* and *Famous* was good enough for the brilliant craftsmen who made this glass, then it is good enough for this author.

Yet when picking a name for an unlisted pattern, you can't just draw it out of a hat. The name you choose must come from the look and the feel of the piece it is assigned to. The name *Leaf Medallion* (Kamm) appropriately described the look of the now-known Northwood line, but the original name *Regent* describes its very presence, its very "aura." How unfortunate that we may never know the original manufacturer's names for many lovely patterns undermined by sterile pattern names.

Thus, I have studied long and hard before finally deciding on names for several of the pieces illustrated in this book. I owe a sincere debt of gratitude to Mr. Joe B. Bell of Memphis, Tennessee, who offered considerable help and advice in providing names for several of the patterns in this book.

THE CONFUSING PRACTICE OF RE-NAMING PREVIOUSLY LISTED PATTERNS

One question which is repeatedly asked me is "Why does a single pattern have to have two names?" No simple answer can possibly come to mind. To investigate the original source of each of the hundreds of different patterns, and check the copyright dates for "priority rights," and then try to ascertain why the second or even third name was introduced by a later author (most of whom are no longer living and cannot be questioned personally) would be time consuming and mostly inconclusive.

But where does the fault lie? Were these early glass authorities deliberately ignoring the previous works of their colleagues? Certainly we are all working toward the same goals—the final accurate listing and attribution of early pattern glass. But to deliberately dub a pattern with their own name, when it was previously named by another writer, is a practice which will be condemned by future generations of glass collectors.

Certainly the honor of having a pattern carry a name which they gave it could not be that important as to create further confusion. The only case where this practice is excusable is when the original name of a pattern has been discovered, a practice I highly praise Mrs. Kamm for undertaking. Today, however, when an original name has been turned up, it should be re-introduced gradually, as there are thousands of more collectors and dealers than there were at the time Kamm re-introduced the original names which she found through her unparalleled research.

The first books on pattern identification appeared in the late thirties, by Dr. Millard (on goblets), Ruth Webb Lee and then Kamm. These three pioneers made attempts at using each other's names, but many cases of avoidable oversights can be pinpointed. Who knows why new names were introduced? Personal reasons could enter highly into it, but this is inexcusable. I myself have endorsed pattern names which I personally condemn for one of many reasons—but you will never see me deliberately re-name a pattern, unless the name is completely wrong for the pattern or continued confusion could be caused by it.

Inadvertently, I accidentally named a pattern in my Book 1, which Kamm had already named in her Book 8. I missed the pattern because she omitted the distinguishable enamel decoration which frequently graced the pattern. I called this pattern

"Optic, Pressed," but I humbly bow to Mrs. Kamm's earlier listing, where she named it "Inside Ribbing." I will be correcting this mistake in the second edition, and I extend my apologies here for my small addition to the creation of further confusion.

For information regarding further corrections and additions to the text of Book 1, see page 103.

THESE PATTERNS WERE _NOT_ MADE IN OPALESCENT GLASS

Due to an understandable mistake, a great deal of confusion has been created over the existence of opalescent pieces in a few patterns. In Kamm 7, plate 55, is a reprint of a page from the Jefferson Glass Company's catalogue, circa 1908. At the bottom Kamm states that the items on that page were an assortment of "pressed colored items with opalescent rims." Mrs. Hartung apparently picked up from this and listed Jefferson's #233 (_Star Rosette_) and #231 (_Double Circle_) as having had opalescent production. As stated earlier, I have studied this Jefferson Glass catalogue personally, and the page referred to here made no mention whatsoever of opalescent production. I personally have never seen nor heard of these two patterns in opalescent, nor have they been reported to me by the dozens of collectors I have interviewed or corresponded with. Apparently Kamm made a little error here which mushroomed into a "collector's dilemma." I don't know how many times I have had collectors ask me to find them just one piece of those two patterns in opalescent to help complete their collection.

Another pattern which has been listed as being made in opalescent glass has not been seen by or reported to me to date. This is Jefferson's #270 (_Jefferson Colonial_) in which again the catalogue never said anything about opalescent production.

So don't believe _everything_ you read, even in this volume. Even the most thoroughly researched book can be found to have flaws, and I look forward to finding about those in mine. I want to learn as much as possible about this exciting early colored glass, and one of the oldest and best ways to learn is from your mistakes.

BUYING, AVOIDING AND INVESTING IN "AS IS" GLASS

Something has come to my attention in recent months about which I felt it necessary to mention in this book. Many dealers are trying to convince customers that a crack or a chip on a piece of glass was "in the making." Oddly enough, this is true more times than not. Only the most astute collector will turn down a rare item which has an imperfection of some kind. But no guidelines have ever been presented before advising collectors of these "manufacturer's flaws."

Listed below are a few signs for you to watch for in deciding whether the piece you find is damaged or a victim of poor workmanship:

1. **Annealing cracks:** These are often referred to as "heat checks" to limit their value destructiveness. These little lines appear usually at the top of the applied handle on cruets, syrups, creamers and water pitchers where they are applied to the body of the piece. Often they have darkened with age, a good sign they are truly "in the making." Most of these cracks did actually occur at the time of production, due to the contraction of the glass as it cooled.

2. **Roughness under the tops of salt and sugar shakers:** Virtually all sugar shakers and many salt shakers are mold blown (not pressed) and were taken off the pontil rod at the top. This often left rough edges, even chips, which the makers saw no need to polish since they would be covered by the screw-top.

3. **Roughness on the top of blown tumblers:** Likewise, tumblers were taken off the pontil rod from the top and then the rough edges were smoothed down. However, frequently small chips went unnoticed, and the tumbler made it to store shelves anyway. These edges are extremely brittle, and highly susceptible to flaking, so if you are holding out for perfect, you'll have a long hard look or will have to buy one professionally polished. The same applies to the berry dishes.

4. **Rough mold lines:** Even pressed glass has its problems, although on a much smaller scale. When the finished piece is removed from the mold, sometimes pieces of glass will stick to the mold and pull glass from the body of the finished piece. This will happen on patterns of intricate design, with many separate raised surfaces (like "Idyll") or on footed patterns (like Swag with Brackets). It takes an expert eye to tell the difference between a real damage-type chip and one from a poor mold job.

5. **Polished bottoms on pressed tumblers:** I have frequently been asked by collectors if certain tumblers in their collections had been professionally polished to remove chips. Although this sometimes proved to be the case, the majority of the time it was not. These pressed tumblers frequently came out of the mold with a lopsided base, which caused the tumbler to lean slightly. They were put to the grinder's wheel to level them off. In some cases, these pressed tumblers were taken off the mold at the base and polished to smooth rough edges. Check the sides of the base. If these have a polished look, _then_ you can suspect professional mending. The above theory also applies to table setting pieces with pedestalled bases. I have seen "Everglades" and "Leaf Medallion" (Northwood's Regent) with polished bases to level them.

6. **Pontil Scars on the rims of opalescent pieces:** The opalescence on many of the novelties was achieved by treating a formed piece of glass with chemicals and then refiring the piece. When the finished product was taken off the rod, sometimes a little scar would remain behind. The _Gonterman Swirl_ opalescent pieces all have little scars on the bottom rim. I have seen several novelties, with scars on the rim where the tool was clamped for refiring. When the tool was removed, the glass usually melted back into shape, but not always. Sometimes a sharp little protrusion of glass will appear to have "dripped" down the glass, and also a deep hole can occur when the glass stuck to the tool, instead of the finished pieces of glass. This should _not_ be considered damage!!!

ATTRIBUTION BASED ON 1905 BUTLER BROTHERS CATALOGUE

Many serious students of glassware have already taken advantage of the reprints which have recently been made available of several of the early Butler Brothers catalogues. This firm was the largest wholesale outlet of glassware from as early as the 1880's to as late as the 1940's. It is interesting to scan these ads and witness the prices that our precious investments originally sold for 70 years ago.

However, Butler Brothers bought the glass outright from the factories and did not name the manufacturers in their ads, so these catalogues appear only mildly interesting. Yet after hours of studying these catalogues for some clues for attribution, it suddenly hit me. Many of the glass "groupings" and "assortments" of pieces contained as many as a dozen different patterns. The ads state that they were packed in barrels for immediate shipment. I suddenly realized that Butler Brothers did not undergo the barrel packing, but the manufacturer. Time after time this theory was substantiated by groupings of "known" patterns. Each assortment contained *known* U.S. Glass patterns, *known* New Martinsville Glass patterns, and *known* Westmoreland Glass patterns, without a single exception.

There is quite a bit of opalescent glassware offered in this 1905 catalogue, and due to these groupings, I have been able to attribute several of the patterns illustrated in this book. We now know the true origins of many of the novelties, which previously remained unattributed or the victims of "guess-work." These include "Palm & Scroll," "Astro," "Wheel & Block," "Keyhole" and "Beaded Fleur-de-Lis," among others. Due to this new found source of attribution, I will gladly buy any old Butler Brother catalogues (heretofore considered not much help in research). If my readers can help me in this quest, I will gladly give them credit in later issues of this series.

GLASS COMPANIES WHICH PRODUCED OPALESCENT GLASS

A.J. BEATTY GLASS CO., Steubenville & Tiffin, O. . . . . Tableware

BEAUMONT GLASS CO., Martins Ferry, Ohio . . . . Table sets, novelties

BELMONT GLASS CO., Bellaire, Ohio . . . . Coinspot, Baby Coinspot

BUCKEYE GLASS CO., Martins Ferry, O. . . . . Blown Opalescent

CONSOLIDATED LAMP & GLASS CO., Fostoria, O. . . . . Blown Opalescent

COUDERSPORT TILE & ORNAMENTAL GLASS CO.,
    Coudersport, Pa. . . . . Novelties, some tableware

DUGAN GLASS CO., (Diamond Glass),
    Indiana, Pa. . . . . Table sets, novelties

FENTON ART GLASS CO., Williamstown, W. Va. . . . . Limited production

A.H. HEISEY GLASS CO., Newark, Ohio . . . . Experimental production,
                                                                                                                            mostly in White Opalescent

HOBBS, BROCKUNIER & CO. (HOBBS GLASS CO.)
    Wheeling, W. Va. . . . . Blown Opalescent

JEFFERSON GLASS CO., Steubenville, O. and
    Follansbee, W. Va. . . . . Tableware, novelties, Blown Opalescent

LABELLE GLASS CO., Bridgeport, Ohio . . . . Blown Opalescent
                                                                                                                            (Northwood associated)

MILLERSBURG GLASS CO., Millersburg, O. . . . . Not substantiated

MODEL FLINT GLASS CO., Albany, Ind. . . . . Table sets, novelties, Blown Opalescent

NICKEL PLATE GLASS CO, Fostoria, O. . . . . Table sets

NORTHWOOD GLASS WORKS, Martins Ferry, O. . . . . Blown Opalescent
NORTHWOOD GLASS CO., Ellwood, Pa. . . . . Blown Opalescent
THE NORTHWOOD CO., Indiana, Pa. . . . . Blown & Pressed wares
H. NORTHWOOD & COMPANY, Wheeling, W. Va. . . . . Novelties, Table sets,
                                                                                                                            and Blown Opalescent

WEST VIRGINIA GLASS CO., Martins Ferry, O. . . . . Blown Opalescent

U.S. GLASS CO., 20 different factories . . . . Continued Opalescent production
                                                                                                                            of Nickel & Beatty; Possibly others.

Also, limited or experimental opalescent production was undertaken by Riverside Glass Co., Wellsburg, W. Va. and McKee Glass Co., Jeannette, Pa. No doubt there were others.

GLIMPSES FROM THE GLASS HOUSES

The following notes appeared in various trade journals regarding the companies which produced opalescent glass. I thought it might interest my readers to scan these for bits of information, just as this author did for clues that might prove important.

January, 1897

"Northwood at Indiana, Pa. specialties are table articles of all kinds, lemonade sets, fancy novelties, and lamps of all sizes and descriptions. These goods are in ruby, blue, crystal opalescent, and various combinations of colors and shades are of the finest lead glass."

January, 1902

"The Beaumont Glass Co. have a pattern which they call No. 106, in plain, rose pink and gold and crystal and gold. They have this in decorated, etched and gold band as well. There are new water sets in crystal, blue, green and ruby, all handsomely decorated. Other things in the exhibit are opalescent novelties in great variety, vases in No. 106 pattern, and numerous miscellaneous articles."

March, 1902 (In reference to National Glass Co.)

"The company has prepared plans for erection of another furnace at the factory in Indiana, Pa. This is the plant where most of the fine colored ware is made, and its product enjoys a prestige equalled by no other in the country."

January, 1904 (at a 1904 Glass Exhibit)

"The name of Northwood is synonymous with high-grade colored glass to everyone in the trade. When Mr. Harry Northwood sold out his Indiana, Pa. plant to the National Glass Co., about two years ago, he went abroad, and the leisure afforded to a man of such artistic tastes, retentive memory and original ideas meant added capital of the richest kind for the new plant, which he opened in Wheeling, W. Va. in May, 1902.

He bought the old Barnes & Co. site, where glassmaking was in vogue in 1830. The new buildings and additions are modern: equipped with the best appliances for his special lines.

Everything in the Northwood display is practically new. There are 125 lemonade sets alone, arranged in a most effective way. The chief feature of the room is several complete lines of tableware, radically different in design and finish from anything in the house. One of these, the Mikado, in frosted glass, with transparent colored enamel flowers artistically trimmed in gold, is novel, almost too novel, but it grows in favor the more it is inspected. The Encore and Regent are regal looking patterns, in several solid colors, rich in heavy gold trimmings."

January, 1904

"Among the most lasting impressions gained by (a buyer's) first round will be the exhibit managed by Mr. George Mortimer, of the Jefferson Glass Company, of Steubenville, Ohio. Not only are the lines exceptionally full, but the arrangement is so good that all its beauty is retained in spite of the inevitable confusion of so much sight-seeing along somewhat similar lines. The number of new patterns in colored lemonade sets, wine sets, toilet ware, etc., is certainly not smaller here than elsewhere, and there are numerous effects in decoration that are both distinctive and in the rarest good taste. The toilet lines, *Iris* and *Vogue*, have a merit that appeals to one instinctively, while the entire display justifies the praise given it by men of discriminating judgement."

April, 1902

"Harry Northwood has made another proposition to the Wheeling Board of Trade relative to securing inducements toward starting up part of the old Hobbs Glass plant. The option given by President D. C. Ripley of the United States Glass Co. on the plant expired April 1, and a conference was arranged to get it renewed. Mr. Northwood proposes to make novelties."

September, 1902

"Harry Northwood is very busy preparing his factory at Wheeling, W. Va., for active work. Everything is being overhauled and put in proper shape and it's expected that operation will begin early next month. Tableware and novelties in crystal, colored and opalescent glass, plain and decorated, will be the product, and in the manufacture of these specialties, Mr. Northwood has few peers, if any at all."

(Month unknown) 1898

"The Northwood Co., Indiana, Pa. represented in New York by Frank M. Miller, is coming prominently to the fore as producers of opalescent and decorated lemonade sets. In these wares, which have long been regarded as a prerogative of the importer, the Northwood Co. is now prepared to make prices which will compare favorably with any asked for foreign goods. The popularity of the Klondyke and Alaska patterns in tableware, which have had such a phenomenal run, would seem by the orders daily received to be unabated. They certainly were original and new, and for next season Harry Northwood promises something that dealers will like even better."

1896 (Month unknown)

"The Buckeye Glass Works, Martins Ferry, recently destroyed by fire, was one of the oldest west of the Alleghenies. It was first established in 1849 and run as a bottle factory for three years with one small furnace. Michael Sweeny, known as the "glass king", was the chief owner and manager for many years. It was known as the Excelsior Glass Works until 1879, when it was changed to the Buckeye. Mr. Seamon has been president since 1884. The cause of the fire is a mystery."

1896 (Month unknown)

"Fires have been drawn in the factory of the Northwood Glass Co., Ellwood, Pa., and no prospects of an early resumption are apparent. Mr. Harry Northwood, who has purchased the large factory at Indiana, Pa., has put fire in the furnace and is prepared to book orders and ship at an early date, all the lines of fine colored and opalescent water sets, novelties and fine lemonade sets formerly made by him at the Ellwood works. New lines of artistic lamps will be put on the market as soon as possible, and early orders for these goods are solicited."

1896 (Month unknown)

"The Northwood Co. is working full hand, and one of the most expert set of off hand workmen to be found in this country are gathered at the works. A fine line of opal tableware, lemonade sets, lamps and colored novelties are being made, and Harry is just letting himself out on fine shapes, color combinations and handsome decorated glassware."

May, 1902

"At this writing—May 5—all but $1,000 of the required $10,000 public subscription has to be raised to secure the plant Harry Northwood proposes to operate in the old Hobbs factory. He intends to make ruby (cranberry) and opalescent ware. The U. S. Glass Co., which owns the Hobbs property, extended the options from April 1 to May 3, and a further continuance until May 8 has been secured. It is known that a small syndicate stands ready to make up the balance of the money, if necessary, so that the scheme is practically assured. Mr. Northwood, who worked in the Hobbs factory in its palmy days, says other towns have made better monetary inducements, but he prefers Wheeling because of its being a better labor market than the smaller communities. This fact actuated his display of patience in waiting throughout the delay. Wheeling never had to cash bonus any industrial proposition before, which accounts for the long time in getting the comparatively small amount."

October, 1902

"John F. Miller, manager of the National's plant at Albany, Ind., and formerly with the Buckeye at Martins Ferry and the Riverside at Wellsburg, was in Wheeling a few days ago and reports the glass business is brisk and all factories in his company working to the limit."

January, 1905

"The name of Harry Northwood is the best evidence that in parlor #6 will be found one of the most frequented exhibits in the house. Mr. Northwood inherits the artistic sense through several generations of glass makers. He not only creates beautiful designs and shapes, but he has a large plant well equipped to quickly produce what the dealer requires. In colored lemonade sets, wine sets, vases, one fire gold decorations and tableware, novelties, ten cent goods, etc., the display is unexcelled. Many buyers think of the output of the concern as chiefly colored ware, but the display of crystal, opal and enamel goods is proof of the variety of pieces made."

October, 1904

"The Jefferson Glass Company continue to bring out goods which attract the instant favor of the trade because of their elegance and quick selling qualities. Mr. Magee, the chief designer and mold maker here, is somewhat responsible for this not unpleasant condition of affairs. His experience at the Heisey works and with other celebrated glass makers has given him ideas and a standard of taste of much practical value. When Mr. C. Grant Fish or his associates, Messrs. Fendt and Mortimer, have a new conception in mind they find Mr. Magee able to produce a mold expressing their best ideas."

September, 1904

"A little more than four years ago Messrs. Fish, Findt, Mortimer and their associates took the present plant of the Jefferson Glass Co. and determined to make a specialty of colored lemonade sets, fine tableware, both colored and crystal, opalescent glassware, vases and novelties of especial merit. They had a good plant, but it was not until about a year ago that they caught exactly what the trade most desired. Since then they have met that want fully and have become leaders in designing some peculiarly attractive goods."

September, 1906

"H. Northwood & Co. are fairly swamped with orders for their new lines. The strikingly beautiful and altogether original 'Verre D'Or' ware in royal blue, amethyst and green, with a massive gold treatment, has taken like wild fire."

"On first sight it looks like a proposition for the jeweler, so heavily encrusted and richly embossed are the gold decorations."

IS ATTRIBUTION REALLY IMPORTANT?

I have asked myself this question a hundred times as I slaved over old journals trying to come up with a long-overlooked ad for a very popular pattern. Since my research for Book 1, I have not had the luck it takes to come up with something "big" to report in Book 2. And that's what it takes—a little dedication, but a **lot** of luck.

Yet is seems the more I learn, the more futile and frustrating this whole research thing becomes. The old expression "Rules were made to be broken" comes to mind. Because, just as I think I have a lead traced down, then something else comes up to put a shadow over the results. I tried to explain the reasons for "dual" and even "triple" attributions in my first book, but they seemed more like weak excuses to me at the time. Now I know for a fact that it is virtually impossible to say "Northwood" made this, or "Jefferson made that." For just as soon as I do, around the corner I trip over a new lead which disproves my claim.

I explained before that my primary technique for glass attribution is through a detailed and careful study of pattern, glass, color and decoration techniques. The best method is naturally through old glass company catalogues and early journal ads. But even these prove to be confusing—the reasons outlined in Book 1. But my own so-called "fool-proof" system seems to be crumbling before my eyes. I will find a decoration technique used on a known Northwood pattern, only to find it later on a known McKee pattern.

This can be explained in a number of ways also, but the simplest explanation is that there was a tremendous amount of transferring of molds and deliberate copying by competitors. It's as simple as that. The primary causes of "attribution headaches" are listed below.

ALBANY GLASS OR NORTHWOOD?

These two companies are reportedly responsible for no less than a dozen patterns and novelties of identical characteristics. Hartung names patterns "Shell & Wreath" and "Ribbed Basket", identifying them as 1903 products of Northwood (referring to an ad she has). Yet 18 years before Dr. Herrick named these patterns "Wreath & Shell" and "Ribbed Spiral," and included them in her 1959 volume on Greentown Glass, attributing these patterns to the Albany, Indiana plant of the Model Flint Glass Co. Shards have been unearthed at the old plant site.

This same double-decker confusion goes for many blown and pressed novelties. The production dates are almost identical, so the logical answer is that the National Glass Company, which purchased both companies in 1899, had the molds transferred from Albany after the company burned around 1902, to Northwood's Indiana, Pa. plant. However, it should be noted here that Northwood was no longer associated with the company at the time, as he was involved with establishing a new company at Wheeling, W. Va. Yet the company no doubt employed many decorators and glass craftsmen who had that distinguishable "Northwood touch."

NORTHWOOD OR DUGAN GLASS?

It is known that the Dugan Glass Company, the offspring of the Indiana, Pa. Northwood plant, continued to produce quality colored tableware and novelties. This interesting note appeared in a June, 1904 issue of "Glass & Pottery World."

"The Dugan Glass Works is manufacturing much the same lines of Bohemian ware as are now made by Harry Northwood at Wheeling. Mr. Northwood had established a great popularity for his lemonade sets and kindred colored glass goods at the time he sold this plant to the National Glass Company. Mr. Dugan has maintained the quality of the famous ware and held much of the trade."

Thus, it appears likely that many pieces which appear in this book might likely have been made by Dugan, using old molds acquired during the takeover of the Northwood plant. This would likely include patterns like S-Repeat, Nestor, Beaded Ovals in Sand. Perhaps we will never know. However, since Mr. Northwood was responsible for the introduction, the design, or the influence necessary to maintain the quality, then he duly deserves credit for these patterns.

JEFFERSON GLASS OR NORTHWOOD?

I have searched long and hard for some connection between these two companies. The similarity in their products after 1900 is staggering. Both produced fine custard tableware. Both produced a large assortment of opalescent novelties and vases. Both put out attractively ornate patterns, frequently enamel decorated. They were only a few miles apart. Yet I can find only one connection.

This connection is a long overlooked passage which I found in a 1904 trade journal which quoted Mr. Northwood as having to keep busy thinking up new designs and ideas for selling his wares which were being produced by his "babies" at Martins Ferry, O., Indiana, Pa. and Steubenville, Ohio. Apparently he retained considerable influence over his two previous plants, but the connection with a Steubenville factory remains somewhat mysterious.

We find some patterns introduced by Jefferson which were later produced in carnival glass by Northwood. Was this some form of trade or payment of debt. Did Mr. Northwood "job out" his iridescent formula for his competitors? This seems hardly likely, since the "Fine-cut & Roses" pattern, first made by Jefferson, can be found in carnival glass signed with a Northwood trademark. This would have required additional mold carving to include this "N-in-a-Circle." Another pattern of similar confusion would be "Ruffles & Rings."

Apparently Mr. Northwood had a much bigger influence on the production of colored glass by his seemingly competitive associates than previously assumed. Until further research turns up some more answers (which will be reported in a later volume), we can only make the above assumptions.

HOBBS OR BEAUMONT?

This one can be a real headache because Beaumont Glass Co., owned and operated by Northwood's brother-in-law, purchased a good number of discontinued Hobbs, Brockunier molds around 1898. The old Hobbs plant was closed after the U. S. Glass takeover, and many of the molds were sold. The blown patterns which were made by both companies include "Seaweed," "Coinspot," "Fern," "Stars & Stripes," "Windows," and "Swirl." Hobbs made these patterns from circa 1888 to 1892. Beaumont reissued them from around 1898 to as late as 1904.

However, whether Hobbs or Beaumont, they were produced with mutual quality of craftsmanship, and the difference in dates seems unimportant to me.

HOBBS OR NORTHWOOD?

Harry Northwood reopened the long-idle Hobbs Glass plant in late 1902. A strong likelihood exists that he may have obtained old Hobbs molds during this takeover, or perhaps even earlier. Certain patterns like "Leaf Mold," "Pillar, Ribbed," "Royal Ivy," and "Panelled Sprig" have finials of identical description (depending upon color). Also, many blown patterns were produced by Northwood after 1902 which were known to have been produced earlier by Hobbs. It should be recalled here that Northwood was very influential in the production at Hobbs, Brockunier when he worked for them during the early 1880's.

BUCKEYE OR MODEL FLINT GLASS?

Much confusion surrounds the dating of these companies wares. Buckeye produced fine colored opalescent wares from 1888 to around 1895. Model Flint Glass Company of Albany, Indiana produced from 1893 to 1902. And yet both are reportedly responsible for "Reverse Swirl."

On page 98 is a reprint of portions of an 1890 Butler Brothers catalogue which definitely predates the Albany glass dates. John F. Miller, associated with Buckeye in 1888, acquired the patent for the process used in making this pattern. And Kamm reports that the piece she calls "Lemon Stripe" was a wedding gift in 1885.

However, shards have been dug up at the Albany plant site. After considerable research I learned that Mr. Miller was manager of Model Flint Glass while it was being run by National Glass. He obviously retained the patents and the know-how he acquired during his Buckeye association, and reissued some of their patterns.

BIBLIOGRAPHY REFERENCES

| BAR | — Barrett, Richard C. | "Popular American Ruby-Stained Pattern Glass" | Forward's Color Productions, Inc., Manchester, Vt. |

BOND — Bond, Marcelle — "The Beauty of Albany Glass" — Publishers Printing House, Berne, Ind.

FREE — Freeman, Larry — "Iridescent Glass" — Century House, Watkins Glen, N.Y.

GODD — Godden, Geoffrey A. — "Antique Glass & China" — A. S. Barnes & Co., Inc., Cranbury, N.J.

HAR CAR — Hartung, Marion — Series of 10 Books on Carnival Glass — Author

HER — Herrick, Dr. Ruth — "Greentown Glass"

HAR OP — Hartung, Marion T. — "Opalescent Pattern Glass" — Wallace-Homestead Co., Des Moines, Iowa

HAR NOR — Hartung, Marion T. — "Northwood Pattern Glass in Color"

KAMM — Kamm, Minnie W. — Series of 8 books on Pattern Glass — Kamm Publications, Grosse Pt., Mich.

LEE EAPG — Lee, Ruth Webb — "Early American Pressed Glass" — Lee Publications, Wellesley Hills, Mass.

LEE VG — Lee, Ruth Webb — "Victorian Glass"

METZ 1 — Metz, Alice H. — "Early American Pattern Glass" — Author

METZ 2 — Metz, Alice H. — "Much More Early American Pattern Glass"

MUR CR — Murray, Dean L. — "More Cruets Only" — Killgore Graphics, Inc., Phoenix, Ariz.

MUR FOS — Murray, Melvin — "History of Fostoria, Ohio Glass" — Gray Printing Co., Fostoria, Ohio

PET SAL — Peterson, Arthur — "Glass Salt Shakers 1,000 Patterns" — Wallace-Homestead Co., Des Moines, Iowa

PET PAT — Peterson, Arthur — "Glass Patents and Patterns" — Celery City Printing, Sanford, Fla.

PRES — Presnick, Rose — "Carnival & Iridescent Glass" — Banner Printing, Wadsworth, Ohio

SM FIN — Smith, Don E. — "Findlay Pattern Glass" — Gray Printing Co., Fostoria, Ohio

SM MIN — Smith, Frank R. & Ruth E. — "Miniature Lamps" — Thomas Nelson & Sons, Inc., New York

TAY — Taylor, Ardelle — "Colored Glass Sugar Shakers & Syrup Pitchers" — Author

UNITT — Unitt, Doris & Peter — "American & Canadian Goblets" — Clock House Petersborough, Ont., Can.

II

Pressed Opalescent Pattern Glass

Listed here you will find the pressed patterns which were made in a table service, with all pieces of identical design—thus the term pattern glass. I have not included the pressed novelties in this section (see Section 4), although many novelties were made in patterns which are also available in a table service.

Some of the patterns you will find listed here were limited to a basic three or four pieces (Frosted Leaf & Basketweave) and others were made in dozens of different shapes (Beatty Rib).

At this writing, these patterns listed here are by far the more collectible of the different types of opalescent glass available. While most collectors start out buying the novelties, their tastes soon advance to the "table service" pieces. They find it a challenge to piece together the "four legs" of a table set, or to find that long-sought sixth tumbler to their water set.

While it may be more effort, it is usually cheaper to reconstruct these sets. It is virtually impossible now to buy a 4-piece table set without paying a premium price. It will take considerable time and patience, but that is what "collecting" is all about. The opposite usually applies to the berry sets and water sets, which usually will cost you less to buy complete than to try and piece together, especially on the more collectible patterns.

FIGURE A

THREE FINGERS & PANEL
(berry)
COUDERSPORT GLASS
(PHOTO COURTESY FLOYD BLISS)

Alaska

(See Pg. 100; Figs. 1-18, Figs. 202 & 217)

Maker: The Northwood Company
Name by: Original manufacturer's name   **Y.O.P.:** from 1897
Colors: crystal, emerald green, white, blue and vaseline opalescent
Decoration: sometimes found with tiny enamelled forget-me-nots with big "elephant ear" leaves—with or without gold
Pieces made: table set, water set, berry set, cruet, banana boat, celery tray (or jewel tray), salt & pepper (see notes below), bride's basket
Pieces not made: toothpick, celery vase
Collectibility: very high, especially among male collectors
Reproduced: No
Important notes: The tumblers and salt shakers are interchangeable with the "Fluted Scrolls" pattern, unless decorated as Fig. 1. The ad reprinted on page 100 introduced these two patterns simultaneously, and is worded as "the two patterns were one and the same." The interchangeable tumbler/salts was obviously a production shortcut. The original cruet stopper is a crystal pressed faceted stopper.

Acorn Burrs & Bark

(See Fig. 153)

Maker: Harry Northwood & Co.   **Name by:** Presnick I, #2
Other name: Acorn Burrs   **Y.O.P.:** circa 1908
Colors: blue, white opales., carnival colors
Decoration: none
Reproduced: No
Pieces not made: salts, toothpicks, cruet, celery, etc.
Collectibility: high in carnival—extremely rare in opalescent, so collectibility can not be established
Interesting note: This author has only witnessed berry sauces in opalescent to date. Undoubtedly a master berry was made. I would be interested in hearing of the existence of any other pieces in this pattern in opalescent.

Argonaut Shell

(See Figs. D, 136, 154, 144)

Maker: The Northwood Company, Indiana, Pa.
Name by: Kamm 4, pg. 32 ("Argonaut")
Original name: Nautilus   **Y.O.P.:** from 1898 to 1910
Colors: blue and white opalescent, novelties in canary opalescent, custard, carnival colors
Signed: script Northwood signature sometimes used
Pieces made: Water set, table set, berry set, cruet, salt & pepper, novelty dishes, toothpick (only in custard), jelly compote
Collectibility: good, but diminished by repro's
Reproductions: By L. G. Wright, in tumbler, berry set, toothpick, salt and pepper—in blue opalescent and custard and crystal and jelly compote
Important: The crystal and opalescent toothpicks found today are all Wright reproductions. Do **not** confuse these for old. See Book 1 for more information on these toothpicks.

Beaded Ovals in Sand

(See Fig. 573)

Maker: Uncertain—possibly Northwood or Dugan, at Indiana, Pa.
Name by: Author   **Y.O.P.:** approx. 1903
Colors: apple green, blue and crystal—rare in opalescent
Signed: No   **Reproductions:** No
Decoration: only on non-opalescent
Pieces made: Water set, table set, berry set, cruet, salt & pepper, toothpick, and a tiny ruffle-edged nappy (illus.)
Unreported items: celery vase, jelly compote
Collectibility: limited—the pattern design is simple, but extremely attractive

Notes: An extremely rare pattern in opalescent colors of white, green and blue. To date I have only witnessed the nappy illustrated (fig. 573), a green tumbler, a blue butter lid and assorted berries in all colors.

Beatty Honeycomb

(Figs. 194, 582-583, 587-589)

Maker: Beatty & Sons, Tiffin, Ohio   **Name by:** Lee VG, pg. 218
Other names: Beatty Waffle   **Y.O.P.:** from 1888
Collectibility: Good, due to rarity
Colors made: blue and white opalescent; no green as reported in Book 1
Pieces made: table set, water set, berry set, cruet, toothpick, celery, salt shakers, mustard, mug, individual creamer & sugar
Pieces not made: rose bowl and pulled vase (these are reproductions)
Reproductions: Yes—rose bowl basket, and vases; green opalescent is not old
Notes: This pattern seems to have had quite limited production. This author has not yet seen the table set, or water pitcher. A collection of this pattern would be most impressive.

Beatty Swirled Opal

(Figs. 50, 63, 64, 186)

Maker: Beatty & Sons, Tiffin, Ohio   **Y.O.P.:** circa 1889
Name by: Kamm 8, pg. 32   **Other name:** Beatty Swirl
Colors made: blue and white opalescent; very rare in canary opal.
Decoration: none   **Signed:** Never
Collectibility: good
Pieces made: table set, water set, berry set, celery, mug, water tray, syrup
Unreported pieces: cruet, toothpick, salt shakers, sugar shaker, mustard   **Reproductions:** No

Beatty Ribbed Opal

(Figs. 129, 213, 585, 586)

Maker: Beatty & Sons, Tiffin, Ohio   **Y.O.P.:** circa 1889
Name by: LEE EAPG, plt. 147   **Other name:** Beatty Rib
Collectibility: moderate   **Colors made:** blue and white opalescent   **Decoration:** None
Pieces made: Table set, water set, berry set (round or rectangular), celery, mug, assorted nappies, mustard, salt shakers, salt dip, cracker jar, sugar shaker, t.p., fingerbowl, match holder
Unreported items: cruet, syrup   **Reproductions:** None
Notes: This pattern apparently sun-purples easily and the blue shade will sometimes have a deep reddish caste. Canary opalescent has been reported previously in this pattern, but remains unseen by this researcher.

Christmas Pearls

(Figure 182)

Maker: Probably Jefferson, circa 1902
Colors & Pieces: only green and blue opalescent cruets have been seen to date; a salt shaker also made.
Other name: *Beaded Panel* (Pet Sal)

Circled Scroll

(Figures 53-62, 581)

Maker: Probably Northwood, at Wheeling, W. V.

Name by: Kamm 4, pg. 70   **Y.O.P.:** circa 1903
Collectibility: Very good
Colors made: blue, green, and white opalescent; later carnival colors
Signed: Never   **Reproductions:** None
Pieces made: Table set, berry set, water set, cruet, salt shaker, jelly compote   **Pieces not made:** toothpick, celery vase
Notes: The attribution is based on the colors made (the green matches perfectly the green in "Wild Bouquet"); also the pattern is strikingly similar to "Beaded Circle," a custard Northwood pattern; also the stopper to this pattern's cruet (not illus.), is the same one used on the "S Repeat" cruet (ref. Unitt, pg. 331)

Colonial Stairsteps

(Figure 576)
Maker: Northwood   **Name by:** Author
Known colors: crystal, blue opal.   **Y.O.P.:** circa 1906
Collectibility: minimal   **Signed:** No
Reproductions: No
Pieces known made: toothpick holder, creamer & sugar
Notes: The creamer & sugar have been reported signed.

Curtain Call

(Figure 170)
Maker: Possibly McKee Glass Co., Jeanette, Pa.
Y.O.P.: circa 1905   **Name by:** Author
Reproduced: No   **Signed:** No
Colors made: known in crystal and very rare in cobalt blue opalescent
Note: Attribution is based on the stopper to the oil bottle, which is in the "Sunk Honeycomb" pattern, a known McKee pattern. The pattern on the caster set is not shown in the McKee book, but this set probably had such limited production that it was not included in a general catalogue.

Daisy & Greek Key

(See Fig. 101)
Maker: Uncertain—reportedly Canadian
Y.O.P.: circa 1900   **Name by:** Author
Colors: white, blue opalescent
Note: only sauces known

Diamond Spearhead

(Figures 130, 179, 192, 212, 584)
Maker: Northwood-Dugan, Indiana, Pa.
Name by: PET SAL, Pg. 159-B
Y.O.P.: circa 1900   **Collectibility:** growing rapidly
Signed: No   **Reproductions:** No
Colors made: green, vaseline, sapphire blue, cobalt blue and white opalescent; also made in crystal
Pieces made: Table set, water set (goblets or tumblers), berry set, toothpick, syrup, mug, celery vase, salt shaker, jelly compote, tankard creamer, high standard compote, cup & saucer
Pieces not known: Cruet, mustard, sugar shaker
Notes: shards unearthed at Indiana, Pa. See Book 3 for further information.

Dolly Madison

(Fig. 138)
Maker: Jefferson Glass Co., Follansbee, W. Va.
Y.O.P.: circa 1907   **Name by:** Author
Other name: Jefferson #271 (Kamm 7, pg. 40)

Colors made: green, blue and white opalescent; crystal & electric blue
Pieces made: table set, water set, berry set
Pieces not made: cruet, salt shaker, toothpick, syrup, celery, etc.
Reproductions: None   **Collectibility:** Good, due to rarity
Notes: Due to the late production date of this pattern, the number of table pieces made was considerably minimized. The name was supplied by this author because there has been considerable confusion over Jefferson's 251 & 271; thus I felt a name was warranted. The pattern is basically a "Colonial" type pattern with a touch of class (the flower spray), and I thought "Dolly Madison" most appropriate.

Double Greek Key

(Figs. 140, 206-207)
Maker: Nickle Plate Glass Co., Fostoria, Ohio (continued by U.S. Glass)
Y.O.P.: circa 1892   **Colors made:** blue & white opales., crystal
Pieces made: (pressed): table set, berry set, water set, celery vase, pickle tray; (blown): salt shaker, mustard, toothpick
Pieces not reported: cruet, syrup, sugar shaker
Name by: Lee VG, plt. 38   **Reproductions:** None
Collectibility: High, especially among Fostoria (Ohio) glass collectors

Drapery, Northwood's

(Figs. 111-118)
Maker: Harry Northwood & Co., Wheeling, W. Va.
Y.O.P.: circa 1905   **Name by:** Har Nor, pg. 35
Collectibility: very good   **Colors:** Blue & white opal.
Signed: usually, with "N-in-circle"   **Reproductions:** None
Pieces made: table set, water set, berry set, perhaps novelties
Unreported items: no cruet, salt shaker, toothpick, etc. known
Notes: The pattern **must** be referred to as "Northwood Drapery" or "Opalescent Drapery" to avoid confusing with the earlier Sandwich pattern of the same pattern name.

Duchess

(Figure 200)
Maker: Riverside Glass Co., Wellsburg, W. Va.
Name by: Author   **Y.O.P.:** circa 1903   **Signed:** No
Reproductions: None **Collectibility:** Minimal—pattern has been unlisted to date
Pieces made: Water set, table set, berry set, toothpick, cruet, lampshade (illustrated)
Unlisted items: salt shakers, celery vase
Colors made: blue, canary & white opalescent; emerald green with gold; crystal, with frosted panels and enamel decoration
Pattern Notes: The "Duchess" pattern is so strikingly beautiful, that it is sad that so little of it can be found today, especially in opalescent. This author has only seen the lampshade and toothpick holder in the opalescent version, but the entire set was undoubtedly produced in it. The emerald green pieces are more easily found, and are uncanily similar to "Empress," a Riverside pattern, and thus I have named this pattern accordingly. The stopper to the "Duchess" cruet is much like one used on the "Esther" cruet, also a Riverside pattern.

Everglades

(Figs. 19-24, 226-227, 100)
Maker: Harry Northwood & Co., Wheeling, W. Va.
Y.O.P.: 1903   **Name by:** Pet Sal, pg. 160-K
Original name: Carnelian   **Signed:** No
Reproductions: No   **Collectibility:** Very High
Colors made: white, blue and canary opalescent; limited green opal. prod.; custard glass; limited purple slag (primarily salt shakers)

Pieces made: Table set, water set, berry set (banana boat shaped), cruet, salt shaker, jelly compote

Pieces not made: toothpick, celery vase

Pattern Notes: The salt shaker in this pattern has an unusual clambroth effect in the opalescence. which has proven confusing to collectors. The vaseline opalescent shaker appears to be a pale custard glass, but is not. The white opalescent looks exactly like clambroth. The blue opalescent shakers are illustrated in Figure 226.

Fan

(Figs. 127-128, 451)

Maker: Both Dugan Glass Co., and possibly Northwood
Y.O.P.: circa 1904   **Name by:** Har Nor, pg. 70
Signed: sometimes with D-in-Diamond   **Reproductions:** No
Collectibility: good   **Colors made:** white, blue, green opalescent; custard; carnival glass; emerald green & cobalt blue
Pieces made: table set, berry set, water set, gravy boat, assorted novelties   **Pieces not made:** toothpick, salt shakers, cruet
Note: Dugan is not credited with carnival production, but if they did, I don't think this is Northwood

Flora

(Figures 209, 219)

Maker: Beaumont Glass Co., Martins Ferry, Ohio
Y.O.P.: from 1898   **Name by:** Kamm 7, pg. 59
Signed: No   **Repro's:** No   **Collectibility:** Good
Colors made: blue, white & canary opalescent; crystal; emerald green
Decoration: green & white is sometimes gilded abundantly
Pieces made: table set, water set, berry set, cruet, toothpick, syrup, assorted novelty bowls, salt shaker, jelly compote, celery vase
Author's Note: This is an extremely attractive pattern which is very hard to piece together a set. In opalescent, this pattern is scarce.

Flute

(See Figure 141)

Maker: Possibly Northwood or Dugan Glass
Y.O.P.: circa 1908   **Name by:** HAR NOR, pg. 22
Signed: No   **Reproduced:** ?
Note: The butter dish illustrated in this pattern has me baffled. I am not even sure it is the "Flute" pattern, although it has all the characteristics of being the same. The finial on the "Fan" butter matches the finial on this one, and the deep color of blue is similar. I have noticed that Dugan's opalescent blue is always a deeper, richer shade, so this was possibly made by them. Yet still, the glass looks awfully new to me. Could this be a Westmoreland product?

Fluted Scrolls

(Figures 102-103, 105-110, 231)

Maker: The Northwood Co., Indiana, Pa.
Y.O.P.: from 1898 to 1900's   **Name by:** Kamm 2, pg. 119
Original name: Klondyke   **Signed:** No
Reproductions: No   **Collectibility:** Good
Decoration: sometimes with an enamelled band of tiny daisies
Colors made: blue, white and vaseline opales.; novelties in green, custard; also made in crystal: rare in green opal.
Pieces made: table set, water set, berry set, cruet, salt shaker, a tiny 2-pc. epergne, round covered "puff tray" (sometimes called a quarter-pound butter), assorted ruffled-edge novelties in bowls
Pieces not made: toothpick, celery vase.
Important: The salt shakers and tumblers in Fluted Scrolls are the same as those used on the Alaska pattern. There is a distinct enamel decoration used on both of these patterns, and this is the only charac-

teristic which will tell these pieces apart. If it has an enamelled band of daisies, it is F.S. If it has a band of tiny Forget-me-Nots with ivy-type leaves, then it is Alaska. All salt shakers and tumblers in emerald green belong to the Alaska pattern, as Fluted Scrolls was not made to any degree in this color.

A "sister" pattern was made called "Jackson." See notes for important information regarding this identical pattern.

Frosted Leaf & Basketweave

(Figs. 95-98)

Maker: H. Northwood and Co., Wheeling, W. Va.
Y.O.P.: circa 1905
Name by: Author   **Signed:** No
Repro's: No
Colors made: blue and vaseline opales.; possibly white; crystal
Decoration: None
Collectibility: rapidly growing
Pieces made: table set; anything else would be very very rare, as this researcher has not witnessed any other items.
Note: With only the table set known to date, production of this line was undoubtedly limited. Attribution is based on the basket weaving which matches identically the basketweave on "Rose Show" (Fig. 448).

Gonterman Swirl

(Figs. 173-178, 195, 568-569)

Maker: Hobbs, Brockunier & Co., Wheeling, W. Va.
Y.O.P.: circa 1885   **Name by:** Author (see Book I)
Other names: Ribbed Swirl   **Signed:** "Pat'd Aug 4, 1876"
Repro's: None   **Collectibility:** High
Colors made: blue or amber top, frosted or opalescent base
Pieces made: Table set, Water set, Berry set, cruet, celery vase, syrup, lamp shade, toothpick holder (sometimes in a frame)
Other possible pieces: finger bowl, salt shaker, sugar shaker
Notes: The patent date refers to the annealing process whereby two separately formed pieces of glass are attached to form a single item. This pattern was **not** made in 1876!!

Gonterman Hob

(Figure 166)

Maker: Hobbs, Brockunier & Co., Wheeling, W. Va.
Y.O.P.: circa 1886   **Name by:** Author
Repro's: None   **Collectibility:** limited, due to rarity
Colors made: Only witnessed with an amber top and opalescent base; could possibly have been made with a frosted base.
Pieces made: I have only seen the cruet to date, although it is likely that a complete table service was made.
Notes: This pattern is very very hard to find. It was made with the same annealing process used on the "Gonterman Swirl" pattern.

Hobnail & Panelled Thumbprint

(Figures 99, 236-239)

Maker: Possibly Northwood   **Y.O.P.:** circa 1905
Name by: Author   **Repro's:** None
Collectibility: limited   **Signature:** has a circle in the base
Colors made: canary, white and blue opalescent
Pieces made: Table set, berry set, water set—tumblers have no thumbprints
Pieces not made: cruet, salt shaker, toothpick

Hobnail, 4-Footed

(See Fig. 156)
Maker: Unknown **Y.O.P.:** circa 1905
Name by: LEE EAPG, plt. 84 **Signed:** No
Reproductions: None **Collectibility:** Fair
Description of pattern: Pieces are square-shaped with four peg-like feet
Colors made: Canary and white opalescent; deep blue opales.; plain crystal, vaseline & blue
Pieces made: Only the table set reported to date

Hobnail, 3-Footed

(See Over-All Hob)

Hobnail-in-Square

(Figures 157, 495)
Maker: Aetna Glass & Mfg. Co., Bellaire, Ohio
Y.O.P.: circa 1887 **Name by:** Kamm 5, pg. 130
Original Name: Vesta **Signed:** No
Reproductions: Several (see pg.)
Collectibility: OK **Colors made:** primarily crystal, white opalescent: rare in colored opales.
Pieces made: Water set, Table set, berry set, celery vase, salt shaker, assorted compotes.
Pieces not made: Cruet, toothpick holder

Hobnail, Northwood

(Figures 167-168)
Maker: Northwood, Wheeling, W. Va. **Y.O.P.:** circa 1903
Name by: Author (Northwood name *must* be included to avoid confusion) **Signed:** No
Collectibility: limited **Colors made:** Hartung reports all colors made, although this author has only seen white opalescent in every case to date
Pieces made: Table set, water set, berry set, celery, individual creamer and sugar (open), mug
Pieces not made: toothpick
Important notes: According to Lee's EAPG, plate 84, the tumbler to this pattern has nine rows of hobs

Honeycomb & Clover

(See Figure 137)
Maker: Uncertain **Y.O.P.:** Circa 1907
Other Name: Honeycomb & 4-Leaf Clover
Name by: Pres. 1, pg. 48
Colors made: white, blue and green opales.; crystal, emerald green; carnival colors
Pieces made: Water set, table set, berry set, assorted novelties (bowls)
Unreported items: nothing else known, due to late production
Interesting Note: It has been reported that this pattern may possibly have been made by the Millersburg Glass Co., Millersburg, Ohio I hesitate mentioning it here, as it cannot be confirmed by press time. The shape of the illustrated water pitcher and the shape of the Water-lily & Cattails are strikingly similar, as are the shades of green. It should be noted here that Millersburg was established by two of the Fenton brothers.

Idyll

(See Figures 149, 199, 384, 558)
Maker: Jefferson Glass Co., Follansbee, W. Va.
Y.O.P.: circa 1907
Other Name: Jefferson #251 (Kamm 7, pg. 46)
Name by: Har Op, pg. 46
Signed: No **Reproductions:** No
Collectibility: Very good
Colors made: white, blue & green opales.; crystal, apple green, blue
Decoration: sometimes decorated with shiny gold
Pieces made: Water set, table set, berry set, toothpick, cruet, salt shaker (these last three sometimes grouped in a set on a tray); berry sauces were made in both 4-1/2" and 6" diameters.
Pieces not made: Celery vase, syrup, jelly compote
Important: Take care not to confuse this *Idyll* pattern with a carnival pattern vase which Hartung inadvertently gave the same exact name.

Inside Ribbing

(See Book I, pg. 34)
Maker: Beaumont Glass Co., Martins Ferry, O. **Y.O.P.:** 1902
Name by: Kamm 8, pg. 37
Other name: Pressed Optic (see Book 1)
Signed: No
Reproductions: No **Collectibility:** limited
Colors made: white, canary, blue & possibly green opalescent; plain and decorated crystal & canary
Pieces made: table set, water set, berry set, toothpick, cruet, salt shakers, cruet set (on tray), celery vase, syrup
Note: This pattern only had limited production in opalescent, so it would take some time to piece together a collection

Intaglio

(See Figures 45-49, 51-52, 134, 216)
Maker: The Northwood Co., Indiana, Pa. **Y.O.P.:** from 1899
Name by: Original Name
Other name: Flower Spray & Scrolls **Signed:** No
Reproductions: No **Collectibility:** Good
Colors made: white & blue opal.; novelties in canary opales.; emerald green with gold; custard glass
Decoration: opalescent was sometimes goofus decorated on flower
Pieces made: Table set, water set, berry set (look like compotes), cruet, salt shakers, jelly compote, assorted novelty shapes
Pieces not made: celery vase, toothpick, syrup jug

Inverted Fan & Feather

(See Figures 39-44)
Maker: Northwood, probably at Wheeling, W. V.
Y.O.P.: circa 1904 **Name by:** Warman's Milk Glass Addenda
Other name: Fan & Feather **Signed:** only occasional salt shakers
Reproduced: Definitely
Collectibility: The Ultimate **Decoration:** shiny gold
Colors made: Flint and blue opales.; custard; green with gold; some carnival colors; novelties in canary yellow opales.
Pieces made: Table set, water set, berry set; rare in cruet, salt shaker, jelly compote, punch bowl, cups, toothpick
Pieces not made: celery vase, syrup jug
Controversial Note: Considerable research has been undertaken to decipher the true age of the undecorated novelties found in this pattern (rose bowl, lady's spittoon, flared candy dishes). A close check between the original Northwood spooner and the rose bowl surfaced considerable differences in the molds. However, contrary to my report in the first edition of this volume, I no longer feel these novelties are reproductions. Pieces have now been documented for acquisition dates (circa 1910), and shards were unearthed at Indiana, Pa. in canary opalescent.

Iris with Meander

(See Figures 139, 155, 224-225)
Maker: Jefferson Glass Co., Steubenville, Ohio
Y.O.P.: circa 1903   **Name by:** Kamm 6, pg. 63
Other name: Fleur-de-Lis   **Signed:** No
Reproductions: No   **Collectibility:** Good
Colors made: flint, blue, canary, and green opalescent; rare in amber opalescent; crystal, blue, apple green with gold (also amethyst)
Pieces made: table set, water set, berry set (2 sizes of sauces), toothpick, salt shaker, cruet, jelly compote, tall vase, pickle dish, plate
Notes: The amber opalescent was experimental, with no major production. I have only seen a few odd shapes in this color to date. The green opalescent is rare in anything except the toothpick & berry set.

Jackson

(See Figures 104, 230, 577, 410)
Maker: Harry Northwood & Co., Wheeling, W.V.
Y.O.P.: circa 1904   **Name by:** Bramer's "Custard Glass"
Other name: Fluted Scrolls with Flower Band   **Signed:** No
Reproductions: No   **Collectibility:** Good
Colors made: flint, blue & canary opales.; custard glass; novelties in green opalescent (Fig. 410)
Pieces made: table set, water set, berry set, cruet, mini. epergne, candy dish

Jewel & Flower

(See Figures 25-29, 228, 229, 509)
Maker: Undoubtedly Northwood   **Y.O.P.:** Circa 1905
Name by: Kamm 8, pg. 30   **Repro's:** None
Collectibility: Good
Colors made: white, blue & canary opales., decorated with gold
Pieces made: Water set, table set, berry set, cruet, salt shaker
Items not made: Toothpick, jelly compote, celery
Important note: It should be noted here that in more than one case, this author has noted that another butter base other than the one illustrated was used. However, the base illustrated is obviously the more "original" of the two. The other is simple in design with a scalloped rim, and was not opalized.

Jewelled Heart

(See Figures 146, 152, 198, 218)
Maker: Northwood (various locations)   **Y.O.P.:** circa 1898-1910
Name by: Kamm 5, pg. 41   **Signed:** No
Collectibility: Average   **Reproductions:** new items in toothpicks, creamers, covered sugars, goblet
Colors made: white, blue & green opalescent; crystal, blue & apple green
Pieces made: Water set, table set, berry set (round or ruffle-edge, cruet, syrup, salt shaker, cruet set, toothpick holder (many of these not made in opalescent), novelties, plates
Pieces not made: celery vase, jelly compote, goblet, wine
Important: I do not believe the goblet or wine were ever made originally, but could be wrong.

Lustre Flute

(See Figures 240, 241, 387)
Maker: Northwood Glass, circa 1906

Name by: Kamm 4, pg. 96   **Y.O.P.:** circa 1908
Other name: *English Hob Band* (Pres. 2, #87), *Waffle Band*
Colors made: Reported only in white & blue opalescent and carnival colors; other opalescent colors would be rare
Pieces made: Water set, berry set, table set, vases, custard cups

Maple Leaf, Northwood's

(See Figures 211 & 435)
Maker: H. Northwood & Co., Wheeling, W. Va.
Y.O.P.: circa 1903   **Name by:** Kamm 5, pg. 133
Signed: No   **Collectibility:** High
Reproductions: None in opalescent; many in crystal & cobalt
Colors made: Opalescent white, blue & green (known only in jelly compote); custard glass
Pieces made: Only the jelly compote has been reported to date in opalescent, although there is a slight possibility that a few experimental sets may have been produced; in custard, this jelly is very very rare, and a water set, table set, berry set, salt shaker and toothpick were also made.
Pieces not made: Celery vase, cruet
Note: The Northwood name must be included in this pattern's identification.

Over-All Hob

(See Figures 160, 165, 169, 567)
Maker: Nickel Plate Glass, Fostoria, Ohio
Y.O.P.: circa 1892   **Name by:** Kamm 5, pg. 107
Reproductions: No   **Collectibility:** limited
Colors made: white, blue & canary opalesc.; amber, blue & crystal
Pieces made: Water set (Fig. 164 is tumbler to this set), table set, berry set, toothpick, celery vase, mug, finger bowl
Unknown items: I am not certain which salt shakers and cruet went to this set, or if in fact these items were even made in *Over-all Hob*. If they were, they would not be footed.
Note: Production on this pattern was undoubtedly continued by U.S. Glass after they took over the plant in 1892. Sometimes the berry set is triangular in shape.

Palm Beach

(See Figures 119-126)
Maker: Reportedly U.S. Glass Co. (their #15119 pattern)
Name: LEE VG, (pg. 178)   **Y.O.P.:** circa 1905 (in opalescent)
Reproductions: none in opalescent   **Collectibility:** Very good
Colors made: blue and canary opalescent; carnival colors
Pieces made: In opalescent, a table set, water set, berry set, finger bowl (or larger sauce dish), jelly compote
Pieces not made: Mrs. Lee reports a good number of pieces made in crystal, but these are not known in opalescent.
Author's opinion: I find it very hard to accept the U.S. Glass attribution, because the carnival colors are **so** much like Northwood. Also, the figural aspect of the finial and handles on this pattern are also Northwood in nature. Perhaps he acquired discontinued molds from U.S. Glass. It is interesting to note that the series number on this pattern is relatively late, yet the pattern was supposedly introduced in the 1890's, whereas patterns with earlier numbers were introduced after 1900.

Panelled Holly

(See Figures 68, 69, 90)
Maker: Northwood, Wheeling, W. Va.   **Y.O.P.:** circa 1905
Name by: Kamm 2, pg. 59   **Repro's:** No
Collectibility: Superb   **Colors made:** white & blue

opales.; green with gold; crystal; carnival

Pieces made: Water set, table set, berry set, novelty bowls, salt shaker

Pieces not made: toothpick, celery vase, cruet

Note: There has been considerable confusion over the purpose of the spooner to this set. Many refer to it as an open sugar. However, a covered sugar **was** made, but is so seldom seen that many doubt its existence. So many creamers & spooners are seen (yet they are far from common) that it is likely that they were sold as a pair by the barrel, with the spooner serving as an open sugar. All other pieces to this pattern are very rare.

Regal, Northwood's

(See Figures 131, 143, 148)

Maker: Northwood, Wheeling, W. Va.   **Y.O.P.:** circa 1905

Name by: Har Op, pg. 88   **Other name:** *Blocked Midriff*

(Pet Sal)   **Signed:** Sometimes with N-in-circle

Repros: No   **Coll.:** good

Colors made: white, green and blue opalesc.; crystal, emerald green

Pieces made: table set, water set, berry set, salt shaker, cruet

Pieces not made: toothpick, celery vase

Note: *Regal* was not the most ideal choice for a name for this pattern since there were already two others known by that name. Thus, the word "Northwood" or "opalescent" should precede this pattern when identifying. The cruet is very rare.

Ribbed Spiral

(See Figures 80-82, 171-172, 205)

Maker: Model Flint Glass Co., Albany, Ind. & reportedly also by Northwood Glass Co.

Y.O.P.: circa 1902 (Model Flint) & 1903 (Northwood)

Name by: Herrick, pg. 37

Other name: *Ribbed Basket* (Har Op, pg. 89)   **Signed:** No

Repro's: No

Collectibility: Good, especially among Albany glass collectors

Colors made: white, blue and canary opales.; no green was made, as previously reported

Pieces made: Table set, water set, berry set, plates, cups & saucers, toothpick, salt shaker, jelly compote, assorted ruffled bowls, vases of all sizes (from 4" to 36" high)

Pieces not made: cruet, celery vase

Note: Apparently this pattern was part of the National Glass Company output, as both companies above were members of the combine. Hartung does not mention the location of the Northwood factory responsible for production (two were in existence at the time), but we must assume it was the one at Indiana, Pa.

Scroll with Acanthus

(See Figures 65-66, 201, 232)

Maker: Northwood Glass Co., Wheeling, W. Va.

Y.O.P.: circa 1903   **Name by:** Kamm 3, pg. 68

Signed: No   **Repro's:** None

Collectibility: good

Decoration: non-opales. sometimes enamelled

Colors made: white, blue & canary opales.; novelties in green opales. (see Fig. 197); crystal, blue & apple green; purple slag

Pieces made: Table set, water set, berry set, jelly compote, toothpick, salt shaker, cruet

Note: See Book 1 for more information on this pattern; it is interesting to note that the jelly compote seems to be a typical item for experimental color production (see Figures 434-435) at the Northwood Wheeling location.

S-Repeat

(See Figures 67, 132)

Maker: National Glass Co., at their Northwood factory, Indiana, Pa.; production likely continued by Dugan Glass Co.

Y.O.P.: from 1903 to circa 1910

Reproductions: Several—none in opalescent, however

Signed: No   **Collectibility:** Fair—diminished by repro's

Colors made: opalescent blue & white (limited); crystal, apple green, blue, and amethyst—sometimes gold decorated

Pieces made: Table set, water set, berry set, toothpick, cruet, wine decanter, wine glass, celery vase (only the first three sets are known in opalescent), salt shaker, cruet set on tray, punch bowl, cups, jam jar

Author's notes: See Book 1 for more notes regarding this pattern. It can now be confirmed that this pattern was indeed made originally by Northwood, as one of my readers wrote me confirming that his grandfather worked at this plant and gave his mother an *S-repeat* toothpick he brought home from work.

Shell

(See Figures 145, 193, 208, 564)

Maker: Undoubtedly Northwood, at Wheeling, W. Va.

Y.O.P.: circa 1903   **Name by:** Kamm 7, pg. 58

Signed: only in carnival   **Repro's:** No

Collectibility: Very high   **Colors made:** white, green & blue opalescent; crystal, apple green, electric blue, canary yellow; carnival colors

Pieces made: table set, water set, berry set, cruet, toothpick, salt shakers, cruet set on tray (the tray is *S-Repeat*), mug

Pieces not known: celery vase

Important: The original stopper to this pattern cruet is the same as the one found in the *S-Repeat* cruet.

Sunburst-On-Shield

(See Figures 183-185, 190)

Maker: Probably Northwood, Wheeling, W. Va.

Y.O.P.: circa 1905   **Name by:** Kamm 8, pg. 52

Repro's: No   **Collectibility:** fair

Colors made: white & blue opalescent; no green is known as earlier reported; rare in canary opalescent

Pieces made: table set, berry set, breakfast creamer & open sugar; the water set has not been reported, and cannot be confirmed

Note: The Northwood attribution is based on the small creamer & sugar. Many of Northwood's later wares (after 1905) had these little pieces made for the set, especially in his carnival lines.

Swag with Brackets

(See Figures 88-94, 135)

Maker: Jefferson Glass Co., Steubenville, Ohio

Y.O.P.: circa 1904   **Name by:** Kamm 1, pg. 86

Repro's: toothpick (none in opalescent top)   **Signed:** No

Collectibility: Good   **Decorated:** Not opales. pieces

Colors made: white, blue, green and canary opalescent (sometime the latter color has a definite vaseline caste); crystal, amethyst, blue, and an odd yellow-green shade, all frequently gold decorated.

Pieces made: Table set, water set, berry set, toothpick, salt shaker, cruet (one of the few with an original pattern stopper), jelly compote, novelties

Unreported items: celery vase

Author's note: I now have more proof that Jefferson Glass Co. made this pattern, other than the ad reprinted in Book 1. The 1905 Butler Brothers Catalogue shows a grouping of bowls, all of which are known Jefferson products, and included was a *Swag with Brackets* master berry.

Thousand Eye

(See Figures 161-164)

Maker: Richards & Hartley, Tarentum, Pa.; production likely continued by U.S. Glass Co., after 1892 takeover

Y.O.P.: from 1888 to circa 1895 (very popular)

Collectibility: Good

Colors made: Opalescent only in white; plain colors of crystal, apple green, canary, blue and amber

Pieces: Every shape imaginable—some are rare in opalescent

Author's note: Care should be taken not to confuse the "Thousand Eye" pattern for several other similarly designed "Raindrop" type lines. However, these others were not made in opalescent.

Tokyo

(See Figures 133, 150, 235, 513)

Maker: Jefferson Glass Co., Steubenville, Ohio

Y.O.P.: circa 1905   **Name by:** Original company name

Collectibility: Good

Colors Made: white, blue & green opalesc.; plain crystal, blue and apple green, all sometimes gold decorated

Pieces made: table set, water set, berry set, salt shakers, cruet, jelly compote, toothpick holder, vase

Pieces not made: celery vase, syrup jug

Trailing Vine

(See Figure B, pg. 25)

Maker: Coudersport Tile & Ornamental Glass Co., Coudersport, Pa.

Y.O.P.: circa 1903   **Name by** Gaddis "Keys to Custard Glass";

Other name: *Endless Vine* by Floyd W. Bliss in Nov. 1972 "Spinning Wheel" article

Reproductions: None   **Collectibility:** Rare—so, limited

Colors made: white, canary & blue opales.; decorated milk glass and custard glass; blue milk glass; rare in emerald green

Pieces made: Table set, berry set, water set, novelty bowls

Author's note: It is possible that only novelty bowls were made in opalescent. Any table set piece in opalescent would be rare.

Twist

(See Figure 562)

Maker: Model Flint Glass Co., Albany, Ind., while a part of the National Glass Company   **Y.O.P.:** circa 1901

Other name: Ribbed Swirl, Swirl   **Collectibility:** Very good

Colors made: white, blue & canary opales.; crystal, frosted crystal, decorated crystal   **Name by:** Kamm 4, pg. 78

Pieces made: Miniature table set (creamer, sugar, spooner, butter)

Important: This set has been incorrectly attributed to the Greentown glass firm. It most decidedly is not a Greentown product.

Waterlily with Cattails

(See Figures 147, 151, 188, 479)

Maker: Both Fenton Glass Co., Williamstown, W. Va. and Northwood Glass, Wheeling W. Va.   **Y.O.P.:** circa 1905

Name by: Kamm 4, pg. 78

Other name: *Cattails & Waterlily* (Presnick, in an earlier publication)

Colors made: white, blue, green and amethyst opalescent; carnival glass

Pieces made: Table set, water set, berry set, novelty bowls, tri-cornered bon-bon, handled relish, individual creamer & sugar, plates, assorted whimseys.

Pieces not made: cruet, salt shakers, celery vase

Note: This pattern was made in three different varients. Frank Fenton tells me that his father made the version with the beads at the base

of the pattern, and he also confirms that the amethyst color was part of his company's early production. The Northwood version of the pattern is slightly different, and is sometimes found signed with the *N-in-a-Circle* trademark. A carnival version of the water set has a basketweave base on the pattern.

Wild Bouquet

(See Figures 30-38, 191, 222, 223)

Maker: Northwood & Co., Wheeling, W. Va.

Y.O.P.: circa 1903   **Name by:** Metz 1, pg. 76

Other name: *Iris*   **Signed:** Never

Reproductions: None   **Collectibility:** Superior

Colors made: white, blue & green opales.; rare experimental pieces in canary opales.; custard glass

Pieces made: Table set, water set, berry set, cruet, toothpick, salt shakers, cruet set on tray (the tray is the same as Chrysanthemum Sprig's)

Author's opinion: Many collectors prefer this pattern in opalescent without the goofus decoration which originally graced the pattern. However, to this author, removing the goofus decoration (unless it is badly worn off) represents a sad misjudgement. Advanced collectors seem to agree that the original decoration should not be taken off. Do we change Mona Lisa's smile just because it isn't to our liking?

Wreath & Shell

(See Figures 70-79, 83-87)

Maker: Model Flint Glass Co., Albany, Ind. and reportedly also by Northwood Glass Company (plant location unconfirmed by previous report).   **Y.O.P.:** circa 1900-1903

Name by: Herrick, pg. 37

Other name: Shell & Wreath (why do writers switch names around like this?)

Signed: No   **Reproductions:** None

Collectibility: Very good

Colors made: white, blue, canary and vaseline opalescent, sometimes decorated with flowers; crystal and crystal with gold

Pieces made: Water set, table set, berry set, celery vase, toothpick holder, rose bowl, ladies spitoon, cracker jar, salt dip, novelties

Pieces not made: salt shakers, cruet (how unfortunate!!!)

Author's notes: Considerable effort has been undertaken in tracing down the source of the Northwood attribution, but I have continually met with a dead end. Until this source can be confirmed, then we must assume that these two companies made the pattern in a joint effort of the National Glass Co., who owned and operated both factories at the time. It seems unlikely that Northwood deliberately copied a competitor's pattern. See Bond's "The Beauty of Albany Glass" for a reprint of the original 1899 catalogue showing most of the pieces made in this pattern and others.

Wreathed Cherry

(See Figure C, pg. 25)

Maker: Probably Dugan, circa 1908

Name by: Kamm 7, pg. 26   **Signed:** No

Repro's: Many—from the 50's in opalescent; Still being made today in a new toothpick

Note: The creamer illustrated may be a reproduction from the early 1950's that Kamm mentions in her Book 7. However, the age wear on the base is legitimate, the pattern detail is good, the glass is light and has good color. Be very careful when buying. Even I have trouble telling the legitimate from the copy on this pattern. The butter dish has been reported signed with Dugan's D-in-a-Diamond trademark.

FIG. B

Trailing Vine

FIG. C

Wreathed Cherry

(creamer)

Illustrations of

Pressed Opalescent Pattern Glass

FIG. D

Argonaut Shell

(water pitcher)

Alaska

1

2
(tumbler)

3

4
(water pitcher)

5

6

7

8
(spooner)

9
(butter)

10
(sugar)

11
(creamer)

12
(celery tray)
(jewel tray)

13
(salt)

14
(cruet)
(n.o.s.)

15
(pepper)

16
(sauce)

17
(berry)

18
(sauce)

Everglades

19
(spooner)

20
(butter)

21
(creamer)

22
(sugar)

23
(water pitcher)

24
(tumbler)

Jewel & Flower

25
(water pitcher)

26
(spooner)

27
(butter)

28
(sugar)

29
(creamer)

Wild Bouquet

30
(sauce)

31
(berry)

32
(jelly)

33
(tumbler)

34
(water pitcher)

35
(spooner)

36
(butter)

37
(sugar)

38
(creamer)

Inverted Fan & Feather

39
(creamer)

40
(butter)

41
(sugar)

42
(spooner)

43
(water pitcher)

44
(tumbler)

Intaglio

45
(creamer)

46
(butter)

47
(spooner)

48
(water pitcher)

49
(tumbler)

Intaglio

Beatty Swirl

50
(water tray)

51
(sauce)

52
(berry)

(sauce)

Circled Scroll

53
(sauce)

54
(berry)

(sauce)

55
(water pitcher)

56
(tumbler)

57
alt)

58
(jelly)

(pepper)

59
(spooner)

60
(butter)

61
(creamer)

62
(sugar)

Beatty Swirl

Scroll with Acanthus

63
(water pitcher)

64
(sugar)

65
(water pitcher)

66
(jelly)

S-Repeat

Panelled Holly

67
(berry)

68
(spooner)

69
(creamer)

29

Wreath & Shell
& Other
Albany Glass

70
(celery)

71
(cracker jar)

72
(tumbler,
footed)

73
(water pitcher)

74
(tumbler,
collared)

75
(creamer)

76
(sugar)

77
(butter)

78
(spooner)

79
(toothpi

Ribbed Spiral

80
(jelly)

81
(cup & saucer)

82
(covered
sugar)

83
(lady's
spittoon)

84
(rose
bowl)

85
(sauce)

86
(berry)

(sauce)

87
(bon-bon)

88
(tumbler)

89 (pitcher)

(tumbler)

Swag with Brackets

90

Panelled Holly
(water pitcher)

91
(creamer)

92
(sugar)

93
(butter)

94
(spooner)

Swag with Brackets

95
(spooner)

96
(butter)

97
(sugar)

98
(creamer)

Frosted Leaf & Basketweave

100

99

Hobnail &
nelled Thumbprint
(sauce)

Everglades
(master berry)

101

Daisy & Greek Key
(sauce)

102
(water pitcher)

103
(tumbler)

Jackson
(water pitcher)

104

105
(powder or puff jar)

Fluted Scrolls
& *"Jackson"*

106
(butter)

107
(spooner)

108
(sugar)

109
(creamer)

110
(salt)

111
(spooner)

112
(butter)

113
(sugar)

114
(creamer)

115
(water pitcher)

Drapery

116
(sauce)

117
(berry)

(sauce)

118
(tumbler)

Palm Beach

119
(sugar)

120
(creamer)

121
(butter)

122
(spooner)

123
(tumbler)

124
(pitcher)

125
(sauce)

126
(finger bowl)

Jan

127
(butter)

128
(sugar)

129
Beatty Rib
(celery)

130 (syrup)
*Diamond
Spearhead*

131 (spooner)
N. Regal

132
Repeat
(tumbler)

133
Tokyo
(jelly)

134
Intaglio
(jelly)

135
Swag / Brackets
(jelly)

136
*Argonaut
Shell*
(cruet; n.o.s.)

33

An Assortment . . .

137
**Honeycomb
with Clover**

138
Dolly Madison

139
Iris with Meander

140
Double Greek K

141
Flute

142
**Frosted Leaf &
Basketweave**

143
Northwood's Regal

144
Argonaut She.

145
Shell

146
Jewelled Heart

147
**Waterlily with
Cattails**

148
**Northwood's
Regal**

149
Idyll

150
Tok

151
**Waterlily with
Cattails**
(tumbler)

152
**Jewelled
Heaart**
(sauce)

153
Acorn Burrs
(sauce)

154
Argonaut Shell
(sauce)

155
**Iris v
Mear**
(tumb

Hobnail & Thousand Eye

156	157	158	159	160
bnail, 4 Ft.	*Hobnail_*	*Hobnail*	*Hobnail*	*Over-All Hob*
(sugar)	*in-Square*	(Hobbs)	(Hobbs)	(pitcher)
(non-opalescent)	(barber bottle)		(butter)	

1984317

Thousand Eye

161	162	163	164
(creamer)	(spooner)	(celery vase)	(water pitcher)

165	166	167	168	169
er-All Hob	*Gonterman*	*Northwood's Hobnail*		*Over-All*
(creamer)	*Hob*	(spooner)	(water pitcher)	*Hob*
	(cruet, n.o.s.)			(tumbler)

35

170

Curtain Call

(castor set)

171

172

Ribbed Spiral

(water set)

Gonterman Swirl

173

(syrup)

174

(spooner)

175

(sugar)

176

(pitcher)

177

(tumbler)

178

Gonterman Swirl

(gas shade)

179

*Diamond
Spearhead*

(indiv. creamer)

180

*Finecut &
Roses*

(spooner)

181

*Buttons &
Braids*

(pressed tumbler)

182

*Christmas
Pearls*

(cruet)

183

Sunburst-on-Shield

(covered sugar)

184

Sunburst-on-Shield

(breakfast sugar)

185

(breakfast creamer)

186

Beatty Swirl

(butter)

An Assortment . . .

187
Stripe
(castor set, 5 bottles)

188
Waterlily with Cattails
(pitcher)

189
Stripe
(castor set)

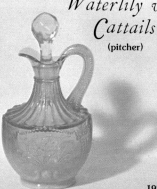

190
unburst - on - Shield
(butter)

191
Wild Bouquet
(cruet)

192
Diamond Spearhead
(goblet)

193
Shell
(butter)

194
tty Honeycomb
(celery vase)

195
Gonterman Swirl
(celery vase)

196
Northwood Block
(celery vase)

197
Scroll with Acanthus
(rare green)

198
velled Heart
(tumbler)

199
Idyll
(spooner)

200
Duchess
(gas shade)

201
Scroll with Acanthus
(canary)

37

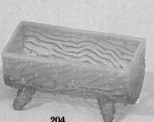

203
N. Town Pump

204
N. Trough

205
Ribbed Sp
(spooner)

202
Alaska
(banana boat)

208
Shell
(creamer)

209
Flora
(butter)

206
(butter)
Double Greek Key

207
(toothpick)

211
N. Maple Leaf
(jelly)

212
Diamond Spearhead
(spooner)

210
Old Man Winter
(small basket)

213
Beatty Ribbed Opal

214
N. Peacocks on a Fence
(salad)

Cruets, Etc. . . .

(PRESSED & BLOWN)

215
(beaumont)
Seaweed

216
Intaglio

217
Alaska
(n.o.s.)*

218
*Jewelled
Heart*
(n.o.s.)*

219
Flora

221
Swag with Brackets

222
Wild Bouquet

223

224

225
Iris with Meander
(n.o.s.)*

227
Everglades
(n.o.s.)*

228

229
Jewel & Flower
(n.o.s.)*

230
Jackson
(n.o.s.)*

231
Fluted Scrolls

232
Scroll with Acanthus
(n.o.s.)*

233
Reverse Swirl
(n.o.s.)*

234
Reverse Swirl
(n.o.s.)*

235
Tokyo
(n.o.s.)*

. = not original stopper

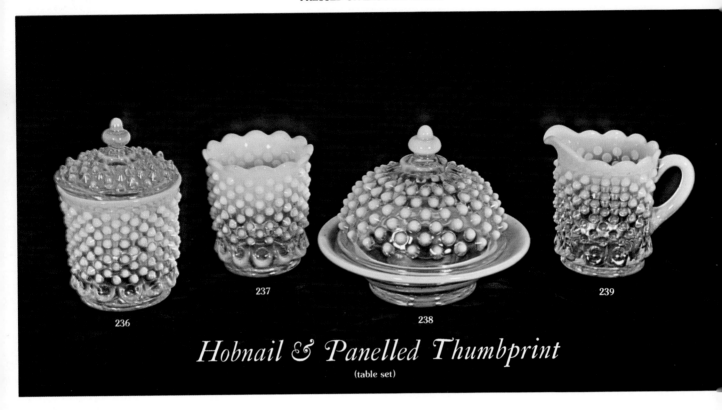

236

237

238

239

Hobnail & Panelled Thumbprint

(table set)

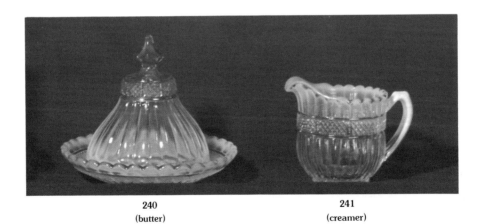

240
(butter)

241
(creamer)

Lustre Flute

III
Blown Opalescent Pattern Glass (text)

This chapter will be the first serious, in-depth study of blown opalescent pattern glass ever attempted. Perhaps the reason for this is due to the futility of presenting accurate data in a field where documented information is virtually impossible to find. I touched upon this subject in Book 1, but was limited by the few toothpicks made in blown opalescent glass. I have continued my research since then, but the irony is that I have managed to uncover more questions than answers.

The reason attributing the makers of each pattern is so difficult is because the competing glass companies deliberately copied each others best-selling patterns. In more cases than one, discontinued molds from one factory were acquired by another, and then reissued.

The *Coinspot* pattern was first made by Hobbs, Brockunier. Then it was made by Belmont Glass, then Buckeye, and later simultaneously by Jefferson, Northwood and Beaumont. So how can a single piece of *Coinspot* be attributed to one of these six different companies? This is where shape, and sometimes color, is the deciding factor. To avoid legal repercussions, these different factories made this and other patterns with slight shape variations from one another.

It is unfortunate that such excitingly beautiful glass has had its value and collectibility minimized because so little documented information has been presented to date. Perhaps this book will bring this long-neglected glass the much-deserved attention it deserves, and bring it to the forefront of collectible glass.

FIGURE E

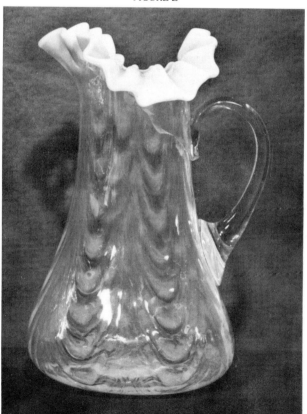

BLOWN DRAPE
COUDERSPORT GLASS
(PHOTO COURTESY FLOYD W. BLISS)

Arabian Nights

(See Figure 266)

Maker: Northwood
Y.O.P.: circa 1895
Collectibility: Good

Name by: Author
Reproduced: No

Colors made: white, blue and cranberry opalescent; rare in canary

Pieces made: Only water set and a syrup jug reported to date.

Notes: This pattern, unlisted until now, is seldom seen for sale today. I have only seen pieces in advanced collections. It undoubtedly had very limited production.

Baby Coinspot

(See Figure 311)

Maker: Belmont Glass Co., Bellaire, Ohio
Y.O.P.: circa 1887
Repro's: See Fig.

Name: Taylor, plate 10
Collectibility: Fair

Colors: This particular syrup has only been reported in white opalescent.

Blown Drapes

(See Fig. 393)

Makers: Northwood, Jefferson, Coudersport & Fenton
Name by: Har Op, pg. 17
Y.O.P.: circa 1900-1910
Collectibility: Fair

Reproduced: No

Colors made: white, blue, green and cranberry opalescent

Pieces known made: water set, barber bottle—tumbler made in pressed form by Fenton, circa 1906

Blown Twist

(See "Twist")

Blue Opal

(See "Fern, Ribbed")

Bubble Lattice

(See Figures L, 298-299, 347-348, 355, 372, 388)

Maker: Hobbs, Brockunier & Co., Wheeling, W. Va.
Y.O.P.: circa 1889
Name by: Author (called "Bubble" in Book 1, Fig. 188)
Reproduced: No
Collectible: Yes

Other name: Plaid (Hartung)

Colors made: white, blue, cranberry and canary opalescent, sometimes with an exciting satiny finish

Pieces made: Water set, berry set, table set, cruet, sugar shaker, syrup, toothpick, finger bowl, salt shakers, bride's basket bowls

Note: See the 1889 Butler Brothers catalogue reprint of this pattern on page 98. I have revised the name only slightly here because the simple name "Bubble" is inappropriate and confusing when applied to the larger pieces, such as the water pitcher.

Bullseye, Opalescent

(See Figures 290, 578)

Maker: Attributed to Hobbs by Oglebay Institute
Y.O.P.: crica 1890
Reproductions: None
Collectibility: fair

Name by: Author

Colors made: Cranberry and white opalescent reported

Pieces made: water bottle, bride's bowl, lamp shades

Note: This pattern is much like *Coinspot* but has heavily raised out "bumps" of opalescence, about the size of a quarter. The spots on *Coinspot* are usually flat and blend in with the glass.

Buttons and Braids

(See Figures 280-282, 181)

Maker: Jefferson Glass Co.'s #182 pattern
Y.O.P.: circa 1905
Repro's: No
Collectibility: Good

Name by: Har Op, pg. 22

Colors made: blue, green and cranberry opalescent; also white

Pieces made: Reported only in the water set, bowls

Note: The tumblers to the set were made in both blown and pressed glass. As mentioned before, the blown tumblers were usually delicate and brittle and highly susceptible to flaking at the upper rim. Perhaps Jefferson (and Northwood) created the pressed version of the tumbler to meet the demands of the consumer. The possibility exists that Northwood may have acquired the Jefferson molds and he created the pressed tumbler, whereas Jefferson made the blown earlier.

Christmas Snowflake

(See Figure 315)

Maker: Hobbs, Brockunier & Co. with reissued production around 1903 by Northwood who acquired many of the old Hobb's molds.
Name by: Author
Collectibility: High

Repro's: None

Colors made: cranberry, blue and white opalescent known

Pieces made: Only the water set

Other name: **Lattice & Daisy** (Har Op); I have replaced this name for two reasons. First, the Hartung name is sometimes confused for the Beaumont syrup "Daisy in Criss-Cross," and second, the name I use has been a popular name for this pattern for years among collectors.

Chrysanthemum Base Swirl

(See Figures 249-254)

Maker: Buckeye Glass Co., Martins Ferry, Ohio
Y.O.P.: circa 1890
Name by: Author's variation on a Peterson name (See Book 1)
Reproductions: None
Collectibility: Good

Colors made: white, blue and cranberry opalescent, sometimes satin finished

Pieces made: Water set, table set, berry set, cruet, syrup, sugar shaker, toothpick, salt shakers, finger bowl, celery vase, straw holder (see cover of book), mustard

Note: The finial on the butter dish (Figure 252) is the same finial found on the *Reverse Swirl* butter (Fig. 314) and the *Seaweed* butter (Fig. "0"). Northwood was associated with Buckeye Glass at this time, and he also obtained the patent for the speckled finish this pattern is sometimes found in. *Chrysanthemum Base Swirl* is attributed by many to Hobb's, Brockunier, but I hope I have presented enough evidence to the contrary.

Coinspot

(See Figures 267-268, 353, 354, 376-379)

Makers: Belmont Glass Co., Bellaire, Ohio (circa 1887)
Hobbs, Brockunier & Co., Wheeling (circa 1888)
Buckeye Glass Co., Martins Ferry (circa 1889)
Beaumont Glass Co., Martins Ferry (circa 1900)
Northwood Glass Co., Wheeling (circa 1903)
Jefferson Glass Co., Steubenville (circa 1905)
Fenton Art Glass, Williamstown, W.Va. (circa 1906)

Name: Popular Nomenclature   **Repro's:** Yes
Collectibility: Good
Colors made: white, blue, cranberry, green, rubina and canary opalescent
Pieces made: Every shape imaginable. Deciding who made a particular piece depends upon the shape of the pattern. The variants are listed below.
Other Name: *Polka Dot* (Hartung); The difference between these two patterns is Coinspot has white dots — *Polka Dot* has colored dots. See Figure 358 for an example of the other pattern.

1. Bulbous-Based Coinspot

(Not Illustrated)

Maker: Hobb's, Brockunier with possible reissued production by Beaumont Glass Company (see notes pg. 15)
Colors: white, blue and cranberry opalescent
Pieces known: sugar shaker (see Figure 263 for shape)

2. Jefferson Coinspot

(See Figure I)

Maker: Jefferson Glass Co.'s #180 (water set) and #83 (salad bowl)
Colors: white, blue, cranberry and green opalescent
Pieces made: water set and ruffle-edged salad bowl

3. Northwood Coinspot

(See Figure 267)

Maker: Northwood Glass, Wheeling, W. Va.
Colors made: White, blue, cranberry & green opalescent
Pieces made: Water set

4. Nine-Panel Coinspot

(See Figures 353, 379)

Maker: Probably Northwood reissue of an old Hobbs mold (this shape is attributed to Hobbs by the Oglebay Institute).
Colors: white, blue, green and cranberry opalescent
Pieces: sugar shaker and syrup jug
Note: The syrup jug was advertised in the 1905 Butler Bros. catalogue, dating the pattern far too late to be Hobbs — at least originally.

5. Ribbed Coinspot

(See Pg. 48)

Maker: Hobbs, Brockunier & Co., circa 1888
Colors: white, blue and cranberry opalescent
Pieces: Water set, salt shaker, probably others
Note: This is a very rare variant of the *Coinspot* pattern. Pieces are on display at the Oglebay Institute in Wheeling.

6. Ring-Neck Coinspot

(See Figures 354, 377)

Maker: Hobbs, Brockunier & Co., Wheeling, W. Va.
Colors: white, blue, cranberry & rubina opalescent
Pieces: sugar shaker, syrup jug

7. Square-Top Coinspot

(See Figure 268)

Maker: Beaumont Glass Co., circa 1900 (possibly made from reissued Hobb's molds)
Colors: white, blue and cranberry opalescent
Pieces: Water set

8. Tapered Coinspot

(Not Illustrated — see Book 3)

Maker: Probably Hobb's, Brockunier
Colors: white, blue and canary opalescent (*Coinspot* is scarce in this last color)

Coinspot and Swirl

(See Figure 306)

Maker: Probably Hobbs Glass Co., Wheeling
Y.O.P.: circa 1890
Colors made: white and blue opalescent reported; rare in amber opalescent
Pieces made: syrup jug and cruet

Consolidated's Criss-Cross

(See Figures 270, 317-319)

Maker: Consolidated Lamp & Glass Co., while at Fostoria, Ohio
Y.O.P.: circa 1888   **Repro's:** None
Collectibility: Good
Colors made: white, cranberry and rubina opalescent, sometimes with a delicate art-glassy satin finish
Pieces made: Water set, table set, berry set, salt shakers, sugar shaker, cruet, syrup, finger bowl, celery vase, mustard, toothpick
Note: In the satin finish, this pattern looks very much like the "Onyx" glass made at Findlay, Ohio. In fact, this pattern is extremely brittle and highly susceptible to flaking, just like the "Onyx" ware. The process by which both patterns were made appears identical.

Daffodils

(See Figures J, 396)

Maker: Uncertain   **Y.O.P.:** circa 1886
Name by: Author   **Repro's:** None
Collectibility: Limited, due to rarity
Colors made: white, blue, cranberry, vaseline and green opalescent;
Pieces made: Water set, syrup, oil lamp — only items seen to date

Daisy and Fern

(See Figures N, 271, 285-287, 297, 302, 307, 341-344, 357, 367-370, 390)

Makers: Buckeye Glass Company, Martins Ferry (circa 1888)

Northwood Glass Co., Ellwood, Pa. (circa 1894)
Northwood Glass Co., Martins Ferry (circa 1890)
Jefferson Glass, Steubenville, O. (circa 1903)
West Virginia Glass Co., Martins Ferry (circa 1894)
Name by: Popular Nomenclature   **Repro's:** Many
Collectibility: Good
Colors made: White, blue, green, cranberry opalescent; reproduced in vaseline (canary) opalescent and other colors
Pieces made: Water set, table set, berry set, sugar shaker, syrup, toothpick, salt shakers, mustard, night lamp, perfume, cruet
Note: As far as I can tell, only Northwood made table set items in this pattern, and only in his *Ribbed Swirl* mold (Fig. 271). The other companies made only water sets and seasoning pieces (syrups, sugar shakers, etc.).

Daisy in Criss-Cross

(See Figures 320-321)
Maker: Beaumont Glass Co., circa 1895
Name: Taylor, plate 11   **Repro's:** None
Collectibility: Good   **Pieces made:** Syrup, water set
Other name: "Daisy Syrup" (Har Op)

Diamonds, Opalescent

(See Figure F)
Maker: Hobbs, Brockunier & Co., Wheeling
Y.O.P.: circa 1888
Colors made: cranberry and rubina opalescent reported
Pieces made: Seen only in water pitchers to date (2 different shapes)

Double Greek Key

(See Page 19)

Fern, Opalescent

(See Figures 296, 300, 350-352)
Maker: Beaumont Glass Co., Martin's Ferry, Ohio (possibly made from old Hobbs molds which they acquired around 1898)
Also made by: Northwood Glass, 1902 (Har Op, pg. 39)
Model Flint Glass, 1900 (Bond, pg. 17)
West Virginia Glass, 1894 (Kamm 5, pg. 89)
Other names: "Blue Opal" (Kamm) and "Fern Sprays" (Har Op)
Reproductions: None   **Collectibility:** Good
Colors made: White, blue and cranberry opalescent
Pieces made: Water set, table set, berry set, sugar shaker, syrup cruet, salt shaker, mustard, celery vase, finger bowl, toothpick, barber bottles, (see Book 1 for more information).

Herringbone, Opalescent

(See Figures 295, 312, 313)
Maker: Hobbs, Brockunier & Co., Wheeling
Y.O.P.: circa 1888   **Name by:** Author
Repro's: None   **Collectibility:** High
Colors made: White, blue and cranberry opalescent
Pieces made: Only the water set and the cruet are reported to date

Hobnail, Hobbs

(See Figures 326-340, 158-159)
Maker: Hobbs, Brockunier & Co., Wheeling
Y.O.P.: From 1885 to 1892
Repro's: Limited reproductions by Fenton
Collectibility: High
Colors made: White, blue, cranberry, rubina, vaseline, rubina verde opal.
Pieces made: Water set, table set, berry set (square shape), cruet, syrup, waste bowl (finger bowl), five sizes of water pitchers, barber bottle, celery vase, brides basket in frame, water tray
Pieces not made: salt shaker and toothpick holder (in opalescent only)
Note: The five different size pitchers should be referred to as (in diminishing orders of height) a lemonade, water, milk, individual milk, and "miniature" water pitcher. Thanks to two devoted readers, Mr. & Mrs. Ed Sawicki, I have learned of the existence of the toy water set in Hobbs' Hobnail. They notified me that the piece that most people considered the toothpick holder (see Book 1, Figure 143) was actually a toy-size tumbler, and they sent a copy of an old Hobbs Glass Co. catalogue to substantiate this claim. I want to personally thank them for this help in my research. The miniature water pitcher is barely 5" tall. This miniature set was only shown in the *Francis Ware* decoration, and no opalescent miniature "sets" were made, although the water pitcher was made (Fig. 339).

Honeycomb, Opalescent

(See Figure G, 275)
Maker: Hobbs, Brockunier & Co., Wheeling
Y.O.P.: circa 1889   **Name by:** Author
Repro's: None   **Collectibility:** Fair
Colors made: cranberry, white, blue and amber opalescent
Pieces made: Water set, cracker jar, syrup seen to date
Note: The unusual color seen in Figure G can also be found in a variant of the *Windows* pattern. I have also seen pieces of *Fluted Scrolls* and *Iris with Meander* in amber opalescent. The pitcher illustrated has an unusual greenish caste at the tope, undoubtedly a reaction from the chemicals in the glass when heated.

Jefferson Drape

(Not Illustrated)
Maker: Jefferson Glass Co., Steubenville, O.
Y.O.P.: circa 1905   **Name:** Har Op, pg. 52
Repro's: No   **Collectibility:** Fair
Colors made: White, blue and green opalescent
Pieces made: Water set only

Leaf Mold

(See Figure 375)
Maker: Either Hobbs, Brockunier or Northwood or both (further research pending)
Y.O.P.: circa 1889   **Repro's:** None
Collectibility: Very High   **Name by:** Taylor, plt. 3
Colors made: rare experimental color of flashed cranberry and opalescent stripes; also made in cased Vasa Murrhina spatter (pink & white), vaseline with cranberry & white spatter (frosted and shiny), frosty camphor-like crystal, blue, cranberry and lime-green, deep cranberry, and opaque colors of white, blue and pink.
Pieces made: Water set, table set, berry set, syrup, sugar shaker, celery vase, salt shakers, cruet, toothpick holder.
Note: As soon as I find this pattern advertised, then dating the glass will pinpoint the maker to better precision.

Onyx, Cranberry

(See Figures 292-293)
Maker: Dalzell, Gilmore & Leighton Co., Findlay, Ohio
Y.O.P.: 1889   **Reproductions:** None
Collectibility: Very very high
Note: The two pieces in cranberry illustrated are very very rare. I am including these highly regarded pieces to illustrate how close opalescent glass is to the "art glass" field. The process used to make Onyx glass was similar to the opalescent process, but the process used on the rare cranberry color is almost identical. However, I do not want to irritate art glass collectors by calling these pieces "cranberry opalescent."

Panelled Sprig, Opalescent

(See Figure 563)
Maker: Known production by Northwood-Dugan at Indiana, Pa.

Name by: Author
Reproductions: Many—in cranberry and "Polka Dot", cruets and salt shakers; also other colors
Colors made: Known only in white opalescent; colored opalescent would be very rare; Plain colors, without the lattice design, were made in cranberry, apple green, amethyst and blue; also rubina.
Pieces made: Opalescent version known only in cruet, toothpick and salt shakers; cranberry and rubina made in a water set, table set, berry set, cruet, sugar shaker, salt shaker (beware of the much darker colored reproductions) and syrup jug; the other colors are only known in the "seasoning" service.
Note: The finial on the butter dish in this pattern is the same one found on the "Ribbed Pillar" pattern (see Book 1, Fig. 233), which seems to substantiate the Hobbs attribution.

Poinsettia, Opalescent

(See Figures 272-273, 278-279, 366, 392, 399)
Makers: Hobbs, Brockunier originally, with the majority of the production undertaken later by Northwood, circa 1903
Name by: Author   **Other name:** "Big Daisy"
Reproductions: None
Colors made: cranberry, blue, white and green opalescent; rare in canary; limited carnival production in pressed tumbler.
Pieces made: Water set, sugar shaker, syrup jug
Note: The water pitcher was made in three different shapes. The tumblers can be found in both blown and pressed glass.

Polka Dot

(See Figures 358, 566)
Makers: Probably Hobbs Glass, circa 1890
West Virginia Glass, Martins Ferry, O. (circa 1894)
Name by: Author   **Other name:** Spot Resist
Reproductions: Yes—Fenton
Colors made: white, blue and cranberry opalescent
Pieces made: Only syrup, sugar shaker, salt shaker & toothpick seen to date; Also a water set (beware of repro's)

Reverse Swirl

(See Figures H, 233-234, 244-248, 284, 291, 303, 314, 572)
Maker: Originally by Buckeye Glass Co., under the guidance of Harry Northwood. Later production by Model Flint Glass Co., Albany, Ind., which was managed by John F. Miller, who earlier worked at Buckeye and who patented the process used on this pattern.

Y.O.P.: from 1888 to 1900   **Name by:** Author
Repro's: None
Colors made: white, blue, cranberry and canary opalescent; sometimes satin finished
Pieces made: Table set, water set, berry set, cruet, toothpick, sugar shaker, syrup jug, mustard, water bottle, finger bowl, salt shaker, custard cup, celery vase, miniature lamp, oil & vinegar cruet set on metal holder (with salt & pepper).
Note: The finials on Figures 252, 255, 314, "O" are identical, and obviously of common origin. The sugar shaker and toothpick appeared in an 1889 Butler Brothers catalog.

Ribbed Opal Lattice

(See Figures 242, 243, 345-346)
Maker: Probably Hobbs, Brockunier & Co., or Buckeye
Y.O.P.: circa 1888   **Name by:** Boul., plt. 195
Other name: Expanded Diamond
Reproductions: None   **Collectibility:** Good
Colors made: white, blue and cranberry opalescent; sometimes the blue has a definite greenish caste
Pieces made: Water set, table set, berry set, cruet, sugar shaker, syrup, toothpick holder, salt shakers, celery vase

Scottish Moor

(See Figure K)
Maker: Unknown   **Y.O.P.:** circa 1890
Pieces known: celery vase, cruet

Seaweed, Opalescent

(See Figures "O", 215, 255-264, 288A, 288B, 389, 579)
Maker: Originally by Hobbs, Brockunier & Co., circa 1890
Molds acquired and reissued by Beaumont Glass, circa 1895
Additional production by Northwood, date unknown
Name by: Author   **Other name:** "Beaumont Beauty"
Reproduced: No
Colors made: white, blue and cranberry opalescent; rare satin finished
Pieces made: Water set, table set, berry set, cruet (2 shapes), syrup, sugar shaker, toothpick (see Book 1) salt shaker, celery vase, miniature lamp, barber bottle.

Spanish Lace

(See Figures M, 276, 277, 308, 322-324, 349, 360, 398, 575)
Maker: originally made in England; major production later by Northwood while at Buckeye & at Indiana, Pa.
Y.O.P.: circa 1888   **Name:** Popular Nomenclature
Reproduced: Not since the 1930's
Other name: "Queen's Lace" (Taylor)
Collectibility: Very high
Colors made: white, blue, canary & cranberry opalescent, very rare in green
Pieces made: Water set, table set, berry set, syrup jug, sugar shaker, celery vase, salt shakers, finger bowl, brides basket, miniature bride's basket, cracker jar, perfume bottle, miniature lamp, water bottle, vases & rose bowls of all sizes & shapes

Stars and Stripes, Opalescent

(See page 110)
Maker: Originally by Hobbs, Brockunier & Co., with reissued production by Beaumont Glass, which acquired old Hobbs molds
Y.O.P.: from 1888 to 1896   **Name:** Har Op, pg. 102
Reproductions: see page 96   **Collectibility:** High

Colors made: white, blue and cranberry opalescent
Pieces made: Water set, barber bottle, lamp shade
Note: The word "opalescent" should precede this pattern's name to avoid confusing it for the pressed pattern of the same name.

Stripe, Opalescent

(See figures 269, 283, 356, 391)
Maker: Primary production by Hobbs, Brockunier & Co.; also by Northwood at Indiana, Pa.
Y.O.P.: from 1889   **Name by:** Author
Other name: "Candy Stripe"   **Repro's:** Yes (see Book 3)
Colors made: white, blue, cranberry, rubina, and rare in canary opalescent
Pieces made: Water set, syrup jug, condiment set, toothpick holder, barber bottle and individual salt shakers seen to date; also a rose bowl
Note: The 4-piece condiment set seen in Figure 189 were advertised in the 1889 Butler Bros. Catalogue, portions of which are reprinted on page 98.

Swastika

(See Figures 309, 310, 359, 397)
Maker: Uncertain   **Y.O.P.:** circa 1895
Name by: Taylor, plate 13
Reproduced: No   **Collectibility:** High
Colors made: white, blue, cranberry and green opalescent
Pieces made: Water set, syrup jug only items reported to date
Note: A very rare and exciting pattern; the water pitcher made in two shapes—a tall tankard style also known

Swirl, Opalescent

(See Figures 294, 301, 304, 305, 325, 373, 380-382, 394, 580)
Makers: Hobbs Glass Co.'s #325, Wheeling (circa 1890)
Reissued by Beaumont (circa 1898)
Jefferson Glass Co.'s #181 (Water set) (circa 1905)
A variant was also made by Northwood-Dugan—See Book 3
(Shards unearthed at factory site in Indiana, Pa.)
Name by: Popular nomenclature
Colors: white, blue, cranberry & green opales.; canary is rare
Pieces made: Water set, table set, berry set, syrup, sugar shaker, 2 sizes of cruets, salt shaker, finger bowl, toothpick, mustard, rose bowl, celery, custard cup, bar bottle, bitter bottle, water bottle, lampshades, cheese dish, finger lamps, cruet set
Note: See the Hobbs Glass catalogue reprint on pages 106-119.

Swirling Maze

(See Figure 274)
Maker: Jefferson Glass Co., Steubenville, O.
Y.O.P.: circa 1905   **Name by:** Author
Reproduced: No   **Collectibility:** Fair
Colors made: white, blue, cranberry and green opalescent
Pieces made: Water set, ruffle-edged salad bowl

Twist, Blown

(See Figures 265, 374, 400)
Makers: Northwood (while at Buckeye and through his own companies)
West Virginia Glass, Martins Ferry (in their "Optic" mold)
Name by: Har Op, pg. 19
Colors made: white, blue, green, cranberry (rare) and canary opalescent
Pieces made: Water set (twisted handle), syrup jug, sugar shaker
Note: This pattern can also be found in the "Nine-Panel" mold, attributable to Northwood

Windows, (Plain)

(See Figure 289)
Maker: Hobbs, Brockunier & Co., Wheeling
Y.O.P.: circa 1889   **Name by:** Boul, plt. 190
Repro's: Yes   **Collectibility:** Good
Colors made: white, blue and cranberry opalescent
Pieces made: Water set, miniature lamp (see page 114), finger bowl, lamps and shades
Note: Reproduced in the water pitcher, tumblers & cruet

Windows, (Swirled)

(See Figures 361-365, 316)
Maker: Hobbs, Brockunier & Co., Wheeling
Y.O.P.: circa 1888   **Name by:** Author (variant)
Repro's: None   **Collectibility:** Good
Colors: white, blue and cranberry opalescent
Pieces made: Water set, berry set, table set, toothpick, mustard, cruet, salt shakers, sugar shaker, syrup (2 shapes), cruet set (pg. 113), celery tray, plates (2 sizes)
Note: This pattern is made from the same molds used on the *Francis Ware Swirl* pattern (see Book 1).

Wide Stripe

(See Figure 395)
Maker: Not certain, but possibly Hobbs, Brockunier
Y.O.P.: circa 1890   **Name:** Taylor, plate 1
Reproductions: None   **Collectibility:** Fair
Colors made: white, blue, cranberry and scarce in green opalescent
Pieces made: Water set (see Pg. 48 for shape), syrup, sugar shaker, cruet, toothpick holder, possibly others
Note: This pattern is also available with a diamond quilt pattern background (See Fig. 395). The hesitancy on the Hobbs attribution is due to the green opalescent syrup I have seen in this pattern. Hobbs did not make green opalescent, to the best of my knowledge. Perhaps the Hobbs molds were re-issued, which is usually the case. See Book 3 for further information.

THE SHAPES OF BLOWN OPALESCENT CRUETS
(Sketches by Adam Scott Gamble)

SHAPE #1
a. opales. stripe
b. bubble lattice

SHAPE #2
(also with ruffled top)
a. seaweed
b. spanish lace
c. swirl
d. daisy & fern
e. coinspot

SHAPE #3
a. seaweed
b. coinspot

SHAPE #4
a. daisy & fern
b. coinspot & swirl
c. royal ivy
d. parian swirl

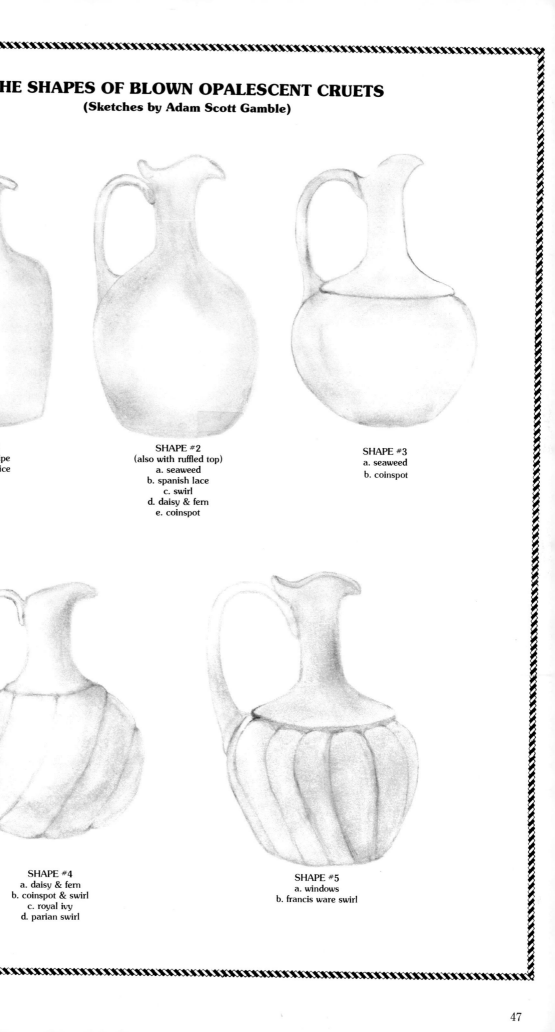

SHAPE #5
a. windows
b. francis ware swirl

SHAPES OF VARIOUS WATER PITCHERS NOT ILLUSTRATED
(Sketches by Adam Scott Gamble)

SHAPE #6
(Hobbs)
a. opalescent diamonds
b. wide stripe
c. Hobbs optic
(Book 1, Fig. 214)

SHAPE #7
(Hobbs)
a. ribbed coinspot
b. ribbed opal lattice

SHAPE #8
a. opalescent fern
(West Virginia Glass Co.,
Martins Ferry, O.)

SHAPE #9
a. opalescent fern
(Model Flint Glass Co.,
Albany, Ind.)
b. opalescent stripe

water pitchers

Fig. F
Opalescent Diamonds

Fig. G
Opalescent Honeycomb

Fig. H (tankard shape)
Reverse Swirl

Fig. I
Coinspot
(Jefferson)

Fig. J
Daffodils
(oil lamp)

Fig. K
Scottish Moor
(celery)

Fig. L
Bubble Lattice
(spooner)

Fig. M
Spanish Lace
(spooner)

Fig. N
Daisy & Fern
(cruet)

Illustrations of
Blown Opalescent
Pattern Glass

Fig. O
Seaweed
(butter)

Ribbed Opal Lattice

Reverse Swirl

244
(tumbler)

245
(mustard)

246
(sugar shaker)

247
(toothpick)

248
(salt shaker)

242
(tumbler)

243
(pitcher)

Chrysanthemum Base Swirl

(unfrosted)

249
(salt)

(pepper)

250
(toothpick)

251
(cruet)

252
(covered butter)

253
(covered sugar)

254
(celery vase)

Opalescent Seaweed

255
(sugar)

257
(creamer)

258 (celery vase)

256
(spooner)

259
(pitcher)

260
(toothpick)

261
(salt shaker)

262
(oil cruet)

263
(sugar shaker)

264
(tumbler)

Pitchers & Tumblers . . .

265
Twist
(blown)

266
Arabian Nights

267
Coinspot

268
Coinspot
(square-top)

269
Stripe
(ring-neck)

270
Criss-Cross
(Consolidated's)

271
Daisy & Fern
(Northwood)

273
Poinsettia
(water set)
(squatty shape)

272

Pitchers & Tumblers . . .

274
Swirling Maze

275
Honeycomb

276 *Spanish Lace* **277**

278
Poinsettia
(tankard shape)

279

280
Buttons & Braids

281

282
Buttons & Braids

283
Opalescent Stripe
(unique opal. handle)

284
Reverse Swirl

285
Daisy & Fern

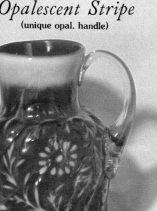

286
(pitcher)

288A   **288B**
Seaweed

289
Windows, Plain

287 (tumbler)

N, Daisy & Fern

290

291

292   **293**

Bullseye
(water carafe)

Reverse Swirl
(creamer)

Onyx Findlay
(vase)   (spooner)

295

296   **297**

299

298

*Opal.
Swirl*
(rubina)

*Opal.
Herringbone*

(toothpick)
*Fern,
Ribbed*

*Daisy
& Fern*
(Apple Blossom mold)

(toothpick)
Bubble Lattice

(finger bowl)
*Windows
(Plain)*

53

300
Opal. Fern
(pitcher)

301
Opal. Swirl
(pitcher)

302
Daisy & Fern
(pitcher)

303
Reverse Swirl
(lamp)

304
Opal. Swirl
(tankard)
(Beaumont)

305
Opal. Swirl
(rose bowl)
(Jefferson)

306
*Coinspot
& Swirl*
(syrup)

307
Daisy & Fern
(optic mold)

308
Spanish Lace
(butter)

309

310
Opal. Swastika
(water set)

311
Baby Coinspot
(syrup)

312
(pitcher)

313
(cruet)

Opal. Herringbone

314
Reverse Swirl
(butter)

315
Christmas Snowflake
(pitcher)

316
Windows
(spooner)

317
(t.p.)

318
(syrup)

319
(t.p.)

Consolidated Criss-Cross

320
(syrup)

321
(tumbler)

Daisy in Criss-Cross

325
Opal. Swirl
(cruet)

322
(salt & pepper)

Spanish Lace

323 (finger bowl)

324
(sugar shaker)

Hobnail by Hobbs, Brockunier & Co.

326
(lemonade pitcher)

327
(water pitcher)
(old reeded handle)

328
syrup
(rubina)

329
(milk pitcher)

330
(celery)

331
(tumbler)

332
(creamer)

333
(bride's basket)

334
syrup
(cranberry)

335
(cruet)

336
(barber bottle)

339
(miniature
water pitcher)

340
lemonade set
(on original tray)

337
(berry bowl)

338
(berry sauce)

Daisy & Fern, N.

341
(cruet)
(Apple Blossom mold)

342
(pickle castor)
(Apple Blossom mold)

343
(toothpick)

344
(cruet)

Ribbed Opal Lattice

Bubble Lattice
(frosted)

345
(cruet)
(frosted)

346
(toothpick)
(unfrosted)

347
(sugar shaker)

348
(toothpick)

Spanish Lace

Opalescent Fern

349
(rose bowl)

350
(syrup)

351
(cruet)

(salt) 352

(pepper)

Blown Opalescent Syrups, etc.

353
Coinspot
(9-panel)

354
Coinspot
(ring-neck)

355
Bubble Lattice·
(unfrosted)

356
Stripe·

357
Daisy & Fern
(optic mold)

358
Polka Dot

359
Swastika

360
Spanish Lace
(old reeded handle)

Opalescent Windows

361
(syrup, tall)·

362
(toothpick)

363
(sugar shaker)

364
(syrup, squatty)·

365
(salt shaker)

·It is notable that these syrups, all attributed to Hobbs, have identical lids.

Sugar Shakers, etc.

366
Poinsettia

367
Daisy & Fern
(Buckeye)

368
Daisy & Fern
(Northwood)

369
Daisy & Fern
(Apple Blossom mold)

370
Daisy & Fern
(alternating panels)

371
Bubble Lattice
(bulbous)

372
Bubble Lattice
(tapered)

373
Swirl
(tall)

374
Blown Twist

375
Leaf Mold

376
Coinspot

377
Coinspot
(ring-neck)

378
(toothpick)

379
Coinspot
(9-panel)

380
(toothpick)

381
Swirl
(short)

382
(toothpick)

Assorted Tumblers

(PRESSED & BLOWN)

383
*Jewel
& Flower*

384
Idyll

385
*Panelled
Holly*

386
Beatty Swirl

387
Lustre Flute

388
Bubble Lattice

389
Seaweed

390
Daisy & Fern

391
Opal. Stripe

392
Poinsettia
(pressed)

393
Drapes
(Fenton)

394
Opal. Swirl

395
Wide Stripe
(diamond quilted)

(rare green)

396
Daffodil

397
Swastika

398
Spanish Lace

399
Poinsettia

400
Twist

IV

Opalescent Novelties

This chapter illustrates and identifies a good number of opalescent glass novelties which originally sold for about a dime at the local variety store. Virtually all of those listed are of the pressed glass category. This author does not like to hear them referred to as "pattern glass," as they were not originally sold as part of an accompanying table service. Because of this, my research in this field is sadly limited.

It is true, however, that many novelties were produced in patterns which were also available in tableware. An example of this would be the *Iris with Meander* pickle tray, and the opalescent pieces of *Trailing Vine* and *Maple Leaf.* Some of these novelties may appear in Section Two.

Opalescent novelties were produced primarily after the turn of the century, from circa 1902 to as late as 1920. Northwood and Jefferson Glass Companies were the major manufacturers, but by no means did they entirely dominate the market. Other companies, such as Beaumont, Dugan, Coudersport, Model Flint Glass, Fenton and possibly Millersburg Glass contributed to the market on a much smaller scale.

Just before press time, I was given the privilege of studying the same Jefferson catalogue which Kamm reprinted in her Book 7. She failed to include several pages which I was given permission to reprint in this Book. However, due to the late date, it was impossible. I will try to include these pages in a later sequel to this volume. The Kamm reprints are rather blurred, and seeing this catalogue first-hand turned up a number of important findings. My sincerest appreciation must be expressed again to the Oglebay Institute for their most kind permission to view this priceless catalogue.

It was interesting to learn the names originally tagged on these novelty pieces, which are all too often today referred to as "candy dishes." In fact, not one piece was referred to by that name in the Jefferson Catalogue. The names by which they were labelled were:

Bon-bon	Fruit Dish	Nappy
Berry	Comport	Nut bowl
Tray	Card Receiver	Cake Plate
Salad	Jelly	Receiver
Handled Olive	Table Dish	Scalloped Dish

No matter what you call your individual pieces today, they were originally used by the Victorian housewife for whatever purpose she saw fit. However, please do not refer to them as "pattern glass."

Due to my limited background in the novelty field, the information offered is considerably less than what you found in the pattern glass sections. I have not tried to name all the different shapes available, because in almost every case a single mold was pulled, flattened, ruffled, stretched, turned in or turned out to form as many shapes as the glass maker could dream up.

My attribution of these novelties is based on several different guidelines. These are:

1. The original Jefferson Glass Co. catalogue in which several novelties were found, many not included in the Kamm reprint.
2. The 1905 Butler Brothers catalogue mentioned on page 11, and other Butler Brothers catalogues reprinted in various publications.
3. If the piece has a cranberry-stained rim, it is most likely a Northwood pattern. I have seen the "Northwood Block" celery vase with this edge.
4. Trademarks—sometimes these novelties are signed with a Northwood *N-in-a-Circle* or a Dugan Glass *D-in-a-Diamond.*
5. If the piece was made with goofus decoration, the likelihood is strong that Northwood made it. He patented this decoration process around 1903.
6. Pattern characteristics—if the feet on an unattributed pattern has the same feet as one whose maker is known, the manufacturer's are probably the same.
7. Color characteristics—this is difficult to depend on in attributing novelties, but it does offer substantiating clues, especially if the pattern was also made in purple slag (*Maple Leaf Chalice*) or custard (*Poinsetta Lattice*) which proves a Northwood attribution.

However, if my research does not turn up enough evidence to name the maker with a certain degree of certainty, then I have left it out. There is too much unsubstantiated guesswork going on as it is, and I don't want my works to create confusion when future researchers turn up the evidence and early catalogues necessary to make accurate attributions.

Abalone

(See Fig. 412)
Maker: Jefferson Glass Co., circa 1903
Name by: Joe B. Bell
Colors made: blue, white, green, possibly canary
Author's Note: See the Jefferson ad reprint in Book 1, pg. 53

Astro

(See Fig. 518)
Maker: Jefferson Glass Co., circa 1905
Name by: Har Op, pg. 7
Colors: white, blue, green, canary (illus.)
Author's Note: This pattern was previously attributed incorrectly to Northwood. However, the 1905 Butler Brothers catalogue mentioned on page 11, reveals this to be a Jefferson product.

Aurora Borealis

(See Fig. 473 & 544)
Maker: Jefferson Glass Co., circa 1903
Name by: Author   **Colors:** white, blue and green opalescent
Note: See the Jefferson ad reprint in Book 1, pg. 53

Autumn Leaves

(See Fig. 492)
Maker: Probably Northwood, circa 1905
Name by: Author
Colors: white & blue opalescent reported; carnival
Note: Presnick calls this "Maple Leaf, Variant" but it does not have that pattern's characteristics—thus the name change.

Barbells

(See Fig. 517)
Maker: Jefferson Glass Co., circa 1905—possible additional production by Northwood
Name by: Author
Colors: white, blue, green & canary opal.; also purple slag
Note: Attribution based on a grouping in the 1905 Butler Brothers catalogue. See page 11 for notes regarding this.

Basketweave Base, Open-Edged

(See Fig. 466)
Maker: Reported to be Fenton by some sources, Northwood by others: I believe it is the former
Name by: combination of *Har Car* & Presnick
Colors: white, blue, green & canary opales.; carnival colors; also cobalt blue

Beaded Cable

(See Figure 467)
Maker: Northwood Glass Co., circa 1904
Name by: Presnick 1, #15
Colors made: white, blue, green & canary opales.; custard; carnival; purple slag

Beaded Drapes

(See Figure 508)
Maker: Probably Northwood, circa 1905
Name by: Presnick 2, #12
Colors made: white, blue, green & canary opales., sometimes with cranberry border.
Note: Attribution is based on this cranberry edge. Known Northwood novelties are found with this unique decoration technique.

Beaded Fan

(See Fig. 515)
Maker: Jefferson Glass Co., #211 pattern, circa 1905
Name by: Presnick 2, #13   **Other name:** Shell & Dots
Colors made: White, blue & green opalescent
Note: The earlier Presnick name for the pattern is retained for two reasons. First, her name for the pattern was from an earlier publication, and I believe in the right of priority. Second, I am trying to clear up the confusion over Northwood's *Shell* pattern which both Kamm & Hartung call "Jefferson's #211," due to a similarity which escapes me. The patterns are not the same at all.

Beaded Fleur-de-Lis

(See Figure 402)
Maker: Jefferson Glass Co., circa 1905
Name by: Presnick 2, #14
Colors made: white, green & blue opalescent; carnival
Note: Attribution is based on the 1905 Butler Bros. catalogue which shows this pattern with a grouping of known Jefferson patterns.

Beaded Star & Medallion

(See Figure 404)
Maker: Reportedly Imperial Glass Co., circa 1910
Name by: Presnick 2, #18   **Other name:** Astral (Har Car)
Colors known: white, green opalesc.; marigold carnival
Note: The Imperial Glass Co., at Bellaire, Ohio, was started by Mr. Edward Muhleman, who earlier was president of Labelle Glass Co., and then the National Glass Company. Perhaps this globe was made earlier in opalescent glass and later in carnival glass at the Imperial firm.

Beaded Stars

(See Figure 424)
Maker: Originally by Bakewell, Pears & Co. (ref. LEE EAPG, plate 190); probably reissued by Northwood, circa 1907
Colors: crystal and opales. white, blue & green
Name by: Har. Op., pg. 10

Beads and Bark

(See Figures 475, 476, 542)
Maker: Northwood Glass, circa 1903
Name by: Har Nor, pg. 35
Colors known: white, blue, green and vaseline opales.; purple slag

Beads & Curly-Cues

(See Figure 506)
Maker: Uncertain   **Name by:** Author
Colors known: white, blue & green opalescent

Berry Patch

(See Figure 454)
Maker: Jefferson Glass Co., #261 pattern, circa 1905
Name by: Joe B. Bell
Colors made: White, blue & green opalescent
Note: This little novelty seemed to escape everyone's attention. It is shown in the rather blurred reprints in Kamm 7, pg. 156, but everyone I talked to assumed that was another piece of *Vintage*. The ad reprint shows a cake plate. Figure 454 illustrates what the catalogue called a "jelly."

Blackberry, Northwood's

(See Figure 481)
Maker: Northwood, circa 1905   **Name by:** Presnick 1, #20
Colors made: blue, white & green.; carnival; custard
Decoration: Frequently found with goofus decoration

Blocked Thumbprint & Beads

(See Figure 463)
Maker: Uncertain   **Name by:** Author
Colors made: white, blue and green opalescent
Note: This pattern is identical to *Leaf Rosette & Beads*, except the flowers are missing here.

Blooms & Blossoms

(See Figure 526)
Maker: Northwood, cira 1908   **Name by:** Author
Colors made: green, white & blue opalescent
Pieces made: novelties in opalescent, emerald green, and carnival; decorated crystal in table set pieces
Note: I discovered this pattern listed by Peterson as "Flower and Bud" too late to list it as such. I have seen carnival pieces signed with an *N-in-a-circle.*

Blossoms & Palms

(See Figure 418)
Maker: Northwood, circa 1905 (reported signed)
Name by: Author
Colors made: green, white, & blue opalescent
Note: Care should be taken not to confuse this pattern with the very similar Northwood pattern, *Shell & Wild Rose.* They are most definitely two different patterns.

Blossoms & Web

(See Figure 489)
Maker: Northwood Glass, circa 1905
Name by: Har Op, pg. 15
Colors made: primarily white opales., frequently with goofus decoration; very very hard to find in colored opalescent

Boggy Bayou

(See Figure 430)
Maker: Uncertain   **Name by:** Author
Colors known: white, blue, amethyst & green opalescent
Note: Made only in vases of all heights and shapes

Bushel Basket

(See Figure 426)
Maker: Northwood Glass, circa 1905
Name by: Presnick 2, #35
Colors made: primarily carnival & custard glass; opalescent white or blue is scarce
Notes: Usually signed with Northwood trademark
Repro's: In all colors (some signed)

Button Panels

(See Figure 482)
Maker: See Notes below   **Name by:** Har Op, pg. 21
Colors made: white, blue and canary opalescent — rare in green opalescent; also made in emerald green, possibly crystal.
Notes: Many dealers and collectors have been buying and advertising this as the *Alaska* pattern. It is strikingly similar, but close inspection reveals a couple of minute differences. The rigaree on the side of the pattern lacks the little feet found at the base of most *Alaska* pieces. Also *Alaska* is usually square or rectangular based, whereas *Button Panel* is round. Finally, this pattern has an interior pattern of faint cross-hatching, not found in *Alaska.*

 Button Panel has been attributed to the Coudersport Tile & Ornamental Glass Co., of Coudersport, Pa. circa 1903. Mr. Floyd W. Bliss, in an article published in the November 1972 issue of *Spinning Wheel,* states that a former decorator from the factory claims that this pattern was made there and was called the "Shadow" pattern.

 However, Hartung states that *Button Panel* was advertised by Northwood, with no dates or actual location offered. Shards have been unearthed at Indiana, Pa., so we must assume the ad dates circa 1902.

Cabbage Leaf

(See Figure 407)
Maker: Northwood, circa 1906   **Name by:** Har Op, pg. 23
Colors made: white, blue and green opalescent; would be rare in canary
Note: A very similar variant of this pattern can be seen in Fig. 406. I named this other pattern *Winter Cabbage*, since it is not as fully leaved as *Cabbage Leaf*.

Calyx Vase

(See Figure 534)
Maker: Both Northwood and Model Flint Glass (Albany, Ind.), possibly due to their mutual association with the National Glass Co.
Name by: Har Nor, pg. 36
Other Name: *Expanded Stem* (Herrick)
Colors made: white, blue & canary opalescent
Note: Herrick's name precedes Hartung's by more than ten years. However the Calyx name has become the more popular and accepted name of the two.

Cashews

(See Figure 461)
Maker: Probably Northwood, circa 1905
Name by: Joe B. Bell
Colors made: white, blue and green opalescent; also goofus glass
Note: Attribution is based on the goofus version of this pattern, which is relatively common.

Carousel

(See Figure 519)
Maker: Jefferson Glass Co., #264 pattern, circa 1905
Name by: Author   **Other Name:** Jefferson #264
Colors made: White, blue & green opalescent

Cherry Panels

(See Figure 441)
Maker: Northwood
Name by: Pres. 2, #49
Colors made: white, blue & canary opalescent; carnival colors
Note: Not Millersburg, as previously reported

Coinspot, Pressed

(See Figure 465)
Maker: Northwood Glass, from 1902
Name by: Variation by Author
Colors made: white, blue, green and canary opalescent; carnival
Note: The word "Pressed" should precede the name of this novelty, to prevent confusing the pattern with the much more popular blown version.

Concave Columns

(See Figure 539)
Maker: Unknown   **Name by:** Author
Colors: white, canary, blue opales.
Note: Reported only in a vase.

Coral

(See Figure 516)
Maker: Probably Jefferson   **Name by:** Har Op, pg. 26
Colors made: white, blue, green and rish canary opalescent
Note: attribution is based on color and pattern characteristics. I am certain it is not Fenton, as previously hinted.

Corn Vase

(See Figures 499, 546)
Maker: Northwood-Dugan, circa 1905
Name by: Har Op, pg. 27
Colors made: white, blue, canary & green opalescent
Note: Beware of reproductions in this pattern. See Fig. 613 for a reproduction piece.

Cornucopia

(See Fig. 484)
Maker: Northwood Glass, circa 1905
Name by: Presnick 2, #35
Colors made: white and blue opalescent reported; carnival

Dahlia Twist

(See Figure 543)
Maker: Jefferson Glass Co., #207 pattern, circa 1905
Name by: Author
Colors: white, blue & green opalescent
Note: This little vase was found in the Jefferson catalogue on a page that Kamm failed to reprint in her Book 7.

Daisy & Plume

(See Figure 419)
Maker: Northwood Glass, circa 1905
Name by: Presnick 1, #52
Colors made: green, white, & blue opalescent; carnival colors

Daisy Dear

(See Figure 439)
Maker: Uncertain   **Name by:** Joe B. Bell
Colors made: white & green opalescent known; blue is likely; carnival

Desert Garden

(See Figure 438)
Maker: Uncertain   **Name by:** Author
Colors made: white, blue & green opalescent

Diamond & Oval Thumbprint

(See Fig. 532)
Maker: Jefferson Glass Co., their #228 pattern, circa 1904
Name by: Har Op, pg. 29
Colors made: white, blue & green opalescent

Diamond's Maple Leaf

(See Figure Q—Also Book 4)
Maker: Dugan-Diamond Glass Co., Indiana, Pa.
Y.O.P.: circa 1908   **Name by:** Popular nomenclature
Repro's: None   **Items made:** only novelties in opalescent

Diamond Point Vase

(See Figure 527)
Maker: Northwood, circa 1908
Name by: Har Op, pg. 30
Colors made: white, blue & green opalescent; carnival

Diamond Point & Fleur-de-Lis

(See Fig. 469)
Maker: Northwood Glass, circa 1906
Name by: Presnick 3, #45
Colors made: white, blue & green opalescent
Note: This pattern is frequently found with the Northwood trademark

Diamond Stem

(See Figure 538)
Maker: Made by both Northwood and Model Flint Glass (Albany, Ind.), undoubtedly due to their common association with the National Glass Company
Name by: Har op, pg. 31
Colors made: canary & white opalescent
Notes: It is claimed that green opalescent is readily available in this pattern, although its existence cannot be confirmed by the dozens of collectors I have interviewed. Blue opalescent may have been made, but it most decidedly would be rare.
    The *Diamond Stem* vase was pulled and flared into several different shapes and may not be easily recognized from the example illustrated in Figure 538.

Dolphin Compote

(See Figure 415)
Maker: Northwood Glass Co., circa 1902
Name by: Har Op, pg. 32
Colors made: white, blue and canary opalescent
Note: Take care when buying this novelty. It has been massively reproduced, and it is very hard to tell the difference. A reproduction compote is shown in Figure 600.

Dolphin & Herons

(See Figure 416)
Maker: Model Flint Glass Co., Albany, Ind., while under the auspices of the National Glass Company; possible additional production at the Northwood, Indiana, Pa. factory
Name by: Author
Colors: white, blue & canary opalescent; crystal
Note: This novelty is made in both a card tray and a vase. The vase is shown in the original National Glass catalogue reprinted in Marcelle Bond's "The Beauty of Albany Glass," page 56.

Dolphin Petticoat Candlesticks

(See Figure 417)
Maker: Northwood-Dugan   **Name by:** LEE EAPG, plt. 143
Colors made: White, blue and canary opalescent
Note: Shards unearthed at Indiana, Pa. factory dump site.

Dragon & Lotus

(Not Illustrated)
Maker: Fenton Art Glass Co., Williamstown, W. Va., circa 1910
Colors made: only white opalescent reported to date; carnival colors; custard
Note: Only the novelty bowl has been seen to date. Obviously very rare in opalescent glass

Dragonlady

(See Figure 486)
Maker: Unknown   **Name by:** Author
Colors made: Only white, blue & green opalescent reported to date.
Note: The rose bowl is illustrated, but undoubtedly novelty bowls and vases were formed from the same mold.

Fan

(See Figure 451)
Maker: Dugan Glass Co., Indiana, Pa. (later Diamond Glass Co.)
Name by: Har Op, pg. 37
Colors: white, blue, green opales.
Note: See also notes under the "Pressed Pattern Glass" section of this book, on page 20. The illustrated novelty in Figure 451, sometimes called a gravy boat, is signed with a D-in-a-Diamond mark.

Fancy Fantails

(See Figure 480)
Maker: Likely Northwood Glass, circa 1905
Name by: Author
Colors made: white, blue, green and canary opalescent, sometimes with a cranberry border
Note: A rose bowl in this pattern is shown in Hartung's Northwood book, page 6, however no mention is made of it in the text. Still, between this and the border decoration, I have arrived at the Northwood attribution.

Feathers

(See Figure 529)
Maker: Northwood Glass, crica 1905
Name by: Har Op, pg. 38
Colors made: white, blue & green opalescent

Fine-Cut & Roses

(See Figures 452, 180)
Maker: Originally by Jefferson in opalescent; later production in carnival and custard glass by Northwood, circa 1908.
Name by: Har Op, pg. 40
Other names: Jefferson's #249 or "Floral & Diamond Point"
Author's Note: It has baffled researchers for years how the molds were transferred from Jefferson to Northwood. These two companies were serious competitors for the colored glass market for over 20 years, both specializing in the same type of glass (except for carnival). Perhaps I will have some clue to the answer by the time the sequel to this book comes out.

Fish-in-the-Sea Vase

(See Figures 531, "S")
Maker: Not definite   **Name by:** Author
Colors made: white, blue & green opalescent, sometimes with goofus decoration on the base
Note: The worn decoration in goofus tends to lean towards Northwood as the manufacturer. The pattern characteristics are very similar to the *Piasa Bird* vase. Both have the bubbles up the side of the pattern.

Fluted Bars & Beads

(See Figures 457, 545)
Maker: Probably Northwood   **Name by:** Author
Other name: "Fluted Opaline Rose Bowl" (Presnick 2, #102)
Colors made: White, blue, green, & vaseline opalescent
Note: Attribution is based on the cranberry border which frequently appears on this pattern. The name of the pattern has been changed from Presnick's earlier name, as her name does little to describe the pattern, and this novelty was formed into shapes other than rose bowls.

Fluted Scrolls with Vine

(See Figure 535)
Maker: Northwood Glass Co., circa 1905   **Name by:** Author
Colors made: White, blue and canary opalescent; would be rare in green

Grape & Cable

(See Figure 497)
Maker: Northwood Glass, circa 1908
Name by: Presnick 4, #68
Colors made: known only in white opalesc.; custard glass; carnival
Note: This pattern, by all rights, should be listed with the pattern glass section, as *Grape in Cable* was made in a complete table service. However, only the punch bowl (Fig. 497) has been reported to date in opalescent, so it should really be considered an experimental piece—a "novelty."

Grape & Cherry

(See Figure 422)
Maker: Uncertain   **Name by:** Har Car 7, pg. 125
Colors made: known only in white and blue opalescent; carnival colors

Grapevine Cluster

(See Figure 503)
Maker: Northwood Glass, circa 1905
Name by: Author
Colors made: reported in blue and white opales.; purple slag
Note: Attribution based on the familiar Northwood purple slag color this novelty is sometimes found in.

Greek Key & Ribs

(Not Illustrated)
Maker: Reportedly Northwood, circa 1905
Name by: Author
Colors made: white, blue & green opalescent; rare in canary; also carnival
Note: The name of this pattern has been changed from *Greek Key* for two reasons. First, there are too many patterns with this same name, and this creates confusion when advertising in trade papers. Second, this pattern was made in two variants, and I felt that they should both have different names.

Greek Key & Scales

(See Figure 423)
Maker: Northwood Glass, circa 1905   **Name by:** Author
Colors made: white, green & blue opalescent; carnival colors
Note: This is a variant of the *Greek Key & Ribs* pattern.

Heart-Handled Open O's

(See Figure 408)
Maker: Northwood Glass, circa 1906   **Name by:** Author
Colors made: white, blue & green opalescent
Note: This is a handled basket in the "Open O's" pattern.

Hearts & Clubs

(See Figure 414)
Maker: Jefferson Glass Co., their #274 pattern, circa 1905
Name by: Author   **Colors:** white, blue & green opalescent
Note: This discovery was found on one of the pages of the Jefferson catalogue which Kamm failed to reprint.

Hearts & Flowers

(See Figure 460)
Maker: Reportedly Northwood, circa 1908
Name by: Har Car 2, pg. 45
Colors made: blue & white opalescent; carnival colors

Heatherbloom

(See Figure 427)
Maker: Jefferson Glass Co., circa 1905—their #268 pattern
Name by: Author   **Colors:** blue, white & green opalescent
Note: This vase was also listed in the Jefferson catalogue.

Hilltop Vines

(See Figure 436)
Maker: Probably Northwood, circa 1907
Name by: Author
Colors: Blue, white and green opalescent

Jefferson Shield

(Not Illustrated)
Maker: Jefferson Glass Company's #262 pattern
Name: Har Op, pg. 56
Colors: white, green and blue opalescent
Note: This is an elusive little pattern, which not one of the many collectors who helped with this project had.

Jefferson Spool

(See Figure 541)
Maker: Jefferson Glass Co.   **Name by:** Author
Colors: white, green, blue and vaseline opalescent

Jefferson Wheel

(See Figure 409)
Maker: Jefferson Glass Co., circa 1905
Name by: Har Op, pg. 57
Colors: white, blue and green opalescent
Note: This was Jefferson's #260 pattern. Presnick calls it "Wheel & Gate" and says it was made in carnival.

Jewel & Jan

(See Figure 437)
Maker: Jefferson Glass Co., circa 1903
Name by: Author
Colors: white, blue and green opalescent; rare in canary
Note: This was Jefferson's #125 pattern. See ad reprint on page 53 of Book 1.

Jewels & Drapery

(See Figures 450, 533)
Maker: Probably Northwood, circa 1907   **Name by:** Author
Colors: white, blue, green and aqua opalescent; possibly carnival

Jolly Bear

(See Figure 490)
Maker: Northwood Glass, circa 1908
Name by: Presnick 3, #114
Colors made: known only in white, blue & green opalescent
Note: The carnival water set with the "dancing" group of bears was made only in carnival glass and is very very rare. Rare in a plate.

Keyhole

(See Figure 432)
Maker: Northwood-Dugan, circa 1904
Name by: Author
Colors made: white, blue & green opalescent

Lattice Medallions

(See Figure 471)
Maker: Northwood Glass Co., circa 1907
Name by: Har Op, pg. 61
Colors made: white, blue, green opalescent
Note: This pattern is sometimes signed with the Northwood trademark. It was incorrectly attributed to Jefferson Glass in an earlier publication.

Laura

(See Figure 487)
Maker: Unknown   **Name by:** Presnick 2, #147
Colors made: white & blue opalescent reported; also carnival

Leaf and Beads

(See Figure 504)
Maker: Northwood Glass Co., circa 1906
Name by: Har Op, pg. 62
Colors made: white, blue & green opales.; carnival, custard glass
Notes: This pattern is sometimes found with the Northwood trademark.

Leaf and Diamonds

(See Figure 493)
Maker: Probably Northwood, circa 1906
Name by: Har Op, pg. 63
Colors made: white & blue opalescent; white sometimes goofus decorated; scarce in green opalescent

Leaf and Leaflets

(See Figure 491)
Maker: Probably Northwood, circa 1908
Name by: Author
Colors made: Reported only in white opalescent, frequently goofus decorated

Leaf Chalice

(See Figure 403)
Maker: Northwood Glass, circa 1903
Name by: Har Op, pg. 64
Colors made: white, blue, canary and rare in green opalescent

Leaf Rosette and Beads

(Not Illustrated)
Maker: Unknown   **Name by:** Presnick 4, pg. 43-P
Colors made: white, blue and green opalescent
Note: The shape is identical to Figure 463, but has a floral pattern.

Lined Heart

(See Figure 536)
Maker: Jefferson Glass Co., circa 1906
Name by: Har Op, pg. 65
Colors made: white, blue and green opalescent
Note: The taller version of this pattern loses its heart-like characteristics, and is not as easily recognized when found.

Lorna

(See Figure 537)
Maker: Model Flint Glass Co., Albany, Indiana, circa 1902
Name by: Author   **Colors:** white, blue & canary opalescent
Note: Sherds of this vase have been dug up at the Albany plant site.

Little Nell

(See Figure 428)
Maker: Unknown   **Name by:** Author
Colors made: blue, white & green opalescent

Many Loops

(See Figure 510)
Maker: Jefferson Glass Company's #247 pattern

Name by: Har Op, pg. 67
Colors made: white, blue and green opalescent

Many Ribs Vase

(See Figure 540)
Maker: Model Flint Glass Co., Albany, Ind., circa 1902
Name by: Author
Colors made: white, blue and canary opalescent

Maple Leaf Chalice

(See Figure 458)
Maker: Northwood Glass Co., circa 1903
Name by: Author
Colors made: white, blue, green and vaseline opalesc.; purple slag
Note: This pattern is constantly being confused for the *Leaf Chalice*, but they are obviously not the same, only vaguely similar.

May Basket

(Not Illustrated)
Maker: The Jefferson Glass Co.'s #87 pattern, circa 1906
Name by: Har Op, pg. 68
Colors: white, blue and green opales.
Note: Every book has its oversight. This basket is not necessarily rare. I just kept overlooking it every time I borrowed from the many collections offered to me. The *Heart Band* toothpick was the "thorn in my foot" in Book 1.

Meander

(See Figure 507)
Maker: Originally by Jefferson, as their #233 pattern, but molds were mysteriously transferred to Northwood around 1908, and the pattern used in carnival production.
Name by: Har Op, pg. 69
Colors: blue, white, green opales.; carnival

Milky Way

(See Figure 498)
Maker: Unknown   **Name by:** Author
Colors: known only in white opales.
Note: This may not be a little novelty. It may be a sauce dish to a berry set. However, I have been unable to find any listing of this pattern in any of the many references available.

Miniature Epergne

(See Figure 474)
Maker: Uncertain   **Colors:** blue, canary opalescent

Netted Roses

(See Figure 425)
Maker: Northwood circa 1906   **Name by:** Har Op, pg. 70
Colors: blue and white opalescent (latter sometimes goofus decorated)
Note: The pattern is often found with the Northwood trademark.

Northern Star

(See Figure 514)
Maker: Undoubtedly Northwood, circa 1910
Name by: Har Car 4, pg. 29
Colors made: white, blue and green opalescent; carnival glass
Note: The large chop plate illustrated is a flattened out mold for a master berry bowl which is more often found in this pattern.

Northwood's Block

(See Chapter II, Figure 196)
Maker: Northwood Glass, circa 1905
Name by: Har Op, pg. 71
Colors made: white, blue, green and canary opalescent, sometimes with a cranberry border on the top rim.
Note: The celery vase was sometimes flattened out into a bowl. No table set pieces were made to accompany this pattern.

Ocean Shell

(See Figure 401)
Maker: Northwood Glass, circa 1904
Name by: Har Op, pg. 73
Colors made: white, blue and green opalescent; purple slag

Opal Open

(See Figure 501)
Maker: Undoubtedly Northwood, circa 1910
Name by: Har Op, pg. 74
Colors made: white, blue, green and canary opalescent
Note: Beware of the reproductions made in this pattern in all sizes and colors, including non-opalescent colors. Also known as *Beaded Panel* (Pres. II, 16)

Old Man Winter

(See Figure 210)
Maker: Jefferson Glass Co., circa 1906   **Name by:** Author
Small Basket: (no feet) Jefferson's #135
Large basket: (footed) Jefferson #91
Note: I have named this pattern due to the resemblance to an iceberg showing the faint features of a man's face, and also since the production date of this pattern coincides with Byrd's discovery of the North Pole. The larger basket usually has a patent date embossed under the rim of the base.

Open O's

(See Figures 524, 408)
Maker: Northwood-Dugan Glass, circa 1905
Name by: Har Op, pg. 77
Colors: white, blue, green and canary opalescent
Note: Shards found at Indiana, Pa. plant site.

Overlapping Leaves

(See Figure 443)
Maker: Undoubtedly Northwood, circa 1908
Name by: Joe B. Bell
Colors made: white, blue and green opalescent
Note: The feet on this unusual cake platter, which unfortunately do not show up in the photograph, are identical to those found on the "Leaf & Beads" piece shown in Figure 504.

Palisades

(See Figures 447, 459)
Maker: Northwood Glass, circa 1905
Name by: Har Op, pg. 78
Colors made: white, blue, green & canary opalescent

Palm & Scroll

(See Figure 431)
Maker: Northwood Glass, circa 1905
Name by: Har Op, pg. 78
Colors made: white, blue and green opalescent
Note: This pattern has been incorrectly attributed to the Jefferson Glass firm. However, the 1905 Butler Brothers catalogue mentioned on page 11 most decidedly leads me to believe Northwood or Dugan made this novelty line.

Peacocks on a Fence

(See Figure 214)
Maker: H. Northwood & Co., circa 1908
Name by: Variation of Presnick 1, plate 149
Other name: Northwood's Peacocks
Colors made: white, blue & cobalt blue opalescent: custard glass, carnival colors
Note: Only the ruffle-edged bowl illustrated has been reported to date. However, an ice cream set is known in the custard and carnival colors, and it is possible that they are available in opalescent as well.

Piasa Bird

(See Figures 446, 530)
Maker: Uncertain, but definitely American
Name by: Author
Other popular names: Old Man of the Sea, Demonic
Colors made: white & blue opalescent
Notes: The name is pronounced Pi-A-Saw. Some sources seem to feel this line is English. I thought so too until recently. The pattern is found on vases, rose bowls, lady's spitoons and rarely on bowls. The bowl illustrated (Fig. 446) is very similar to the Flora novelty bowl in color and shape, which leans toward Beaumont as its manufacturer. Also, the Piasa Bird is an American legendary creature and I have included its picture to illustrate this uncanny similarity of features which led me to naming the pattern after it. My thanks to Don Farrell, Sr. for making me aware of this early Indian legend.

Piasa Bird

Pineapple & Fan, Heisey

(See Figure 442)
Maker: A. H. Heisey Glass Co., circa 1898
Name by: Kamm 2, pg. 93
Other name: Heisey #1255
Colors made: crystal, ruby-stained, emerald green, some custard souvenirs; rare experimental pieces in opalescent glass
Note: Heisey's *Prison Stripe* and *Peerless* patterns also underwent rare opalescent glass production.

Pearl Flowers

(See Figure 456)
Maker: Uncertain   **Name by:** Har Op, pg. 82
Colors made: white, blue and green opalescent
Other name: *Beaded Flower Rosette* (Pres. II, 15)

Pearls & Scales

(See Figure 483)
Maker: Northwood Glass, circa 1905   **Name by:** Author
Colors made: white, blue, green and canary opalescent, often with the distinguishable cranberry-stained border.

Poinsettia Lattice

(See Figure 453)
Maker: Probably Northwood Glass, circa 1907
Name by: Presnick 3, #162
Other name: "Christmas Bowl"
Colors made: white, blue and canary opales.; carnival glass
Note: Presnick attributes this to Fenton. However, just before press time I found a canary opalescent bowl in this pattern and the color was the deepest yellow imaginable, and totally uncharacteristic of Fenton colors. Also, this bowl can be found in custard glass with the same blue stain sometimes found on Northwood's "Grape & Cable."

Popsickle Sticks

(See Figure 522)
Maker: Jefferson Glass Co.'s #263 pattern
Name by: Author
Colors made: white, blue and green opalescent

Pump & Trough

(See Figures 203-204)
Maker: Northwood Glass Co., circa 1907
Name: Common usage
Colors made: white, blue and canary opalescent; reported, but unconfirmed, in a rare green opalescent; also made in emerald green
Important: The pattern has been reproduced, so be careful. Some of the original pumps and troughs were signed Northwood in script, but not all of them, so do not depend upon the signature to determine authenticity. Just compare them to the illustration in this book and that should be enough to tell.

Reverse Drapery

(See Figure 479)
Maker: Probably Northwood, circa 1907   **Name by:** Author
Colors made: blue, white and green opalescent

Reflecting Diamonds

(See Figure 411)
Maker: Northwood, circa 1905   **Name by:** Author
Colors: white, blue and green opalescent
Note: Attribution of this pattern is based on the 1905 Butler Brothers catalogue mentioned on page 11.

Reflections

(See Figure 444)
Maker: Dugan Glass Co., Indiana, Pa. (later Diamond Glass)
Name by: Author   **Colors:** white, blue & green opalescent
Note: This bowl is signed with the D-in-a-Diamond trademark.

Ring-Handled Basket Salt Shaker

(See Figure 571)
Maker: Probably Northwood, circa 1905
Name by: Pet Sal, pg. 37-K
Colors made: Opalescent blue and white, with a clambroth effect similar to the *Everglades* salt shakers seen in Figure 226; also made in opaque colors.

Rose Show

(See Figure 448)
Maker: Most sources attribute this to Northwood; I concur
Name by: Har Car 2, pg. 87   **Other name:** *LaBelle Rose* (Presnick)
Note: The opalescent carnival version of this pattern is shown in Figure 448. I was unable to locate the unirridized version of this bowl by press time, although I had seen it at shows many times before. I have never seen the plate in plain opalescent, and it would certainly be a "find" if it does exist. I have only seen the bowl in blue opalescent and carnival colors.

Roulette

(See Figure 511)
Maker: Northwood Glass, circa 1906   **Name by:** Joe B. Bell
Colors made: white, blue and green opalescent
Note: This pattern is virtually identical to the *Diamond Point & Fleur-de-Lis* pattern shown in Figure 469, a signed Northwood pattern. Thus the attribution.

Ruffles and Rings

(See Figure 512)

Maker: Jefferson Glass Co.'s #208 pattern, with molds somehow transferred to Northwood later for carnival production (1905-1910)
Name by: Har Op, pg. 91
Other name: Carnations & Pleats (Pres. II, 44)
Colors made: white, blue and green opalescent; carnival glass
Note: This pattern was earlier exclusively attributed to Northwood, with no mention of the Jefferson origins. I feel that the Jefferson firm at least deserves recognition for designing this relatively common novelty.

Scheherezade

(See Figure 464)

Maker: Unknown   **Name by:** Author
Colors made: white, blue & green opalescent known

Sea Spray

(See Figure 523)

Maker: Jefferson Glass Co.'s #192 pattern, circa 1906
Name by: Har Op, pg. 93
Colors: white, blue & green opalescent

Shell and Wild Rose

(See Figure 468)

Maker: Northwood Glass Co., circa 1906
Name by: Presnick 1, #174
Colors made: white, blue and green opalescent
Note: Sometimes signed with the Northwood trademark

Simple Simon Vase

(See Figure 433)

Maker: Unknown   **Name by:** Author
Colors made: only seen in green & white opalescent to date; other colors likely

Sir Lancelot

(See Figure 405)

Maker: Northwood, Wheeling, W. Va., circa 1908
Name by: Author
Colors made: green, white and blue opalescent; possibly carnival.

Spokes and Wheels

(See Figure 462)

Maker: Northwood, at Wheeling, circa 1908
Name by: Author
Colors made: white, blue and green opalescent

Spool

(See Figures 449, 472)

Maker: Undoubtedly Northwood
Name by: Har Op, pg. 99
Colors made: white, blue and green opalescent; purple slag; custard
Note: The pattern that Hartung shows as *Spool*, I have renamed *Spool of Threads*, since it has the vertical ribs in it.

Spool of Threads

(See Figure 525)

Maker: Northwood, circa 1905   **Name by:** Author
Colors made: white, blue and green opalescent; purple slag
Note: Hartung calls this "Spool"

Stork and Rushes Mug

(See Figure 500)

Maker: Reportedly Northwood, circa 1910
Name by: Har Car 1-125
Colors known: found only in blue opalescent & carnival colors to date
Note: There are slight variations in the pattern shown here and the pattern shown in carnival books, but the storks are identical.

Strawberry and Dahlia Twist (Epergne)

(See Figure T)

Maker: Fenton Art Glass Co., circa 1910
Colors known: white & blue opalescent; carnival colors
Note: This epergne is included in a Butler Brothers ad reprint shown in Freeman's book "Iridescent Glass," and the base and trumpet vase are original.

Thistle Patch

(See Figure 496)

Maker: Uncertain   **Name by:** Author
Colors: found only in white opalescent to date
Note: This may be the same pattern which Hartung calls *Thistle*, but I cannot tell from her drawing. The piece illustrated as Fig. 496 is a pressed piece, not blown, so they probably are differnt patterns.

Three Fingers and Panel

(See Figure A)

Maker: Coudersport Tile & Ornamental Glass Co., circa 1905
Name by: Floyd W. Bliss
Colors: blue, canary & white opalescent
Note: This is a very hard to find pattern.

Three Fruits

(See Figure 420)

Maker: Northwood Glass Co., circa 1907
Name by: Har Op, pg. 105
Colors made: white and blue opalescent reported to date; carnival
Note: See also Figure 421.

Three Fruits with Meander

(See Figure 421)

Maker: Northwood Glass, circa 1907   **Name by:** Author
Colors made: white and blue opalescent; carnival glass
Note: The *Meander* pattern is on the bottom side of the bowl and can be seen by turning the bowl over.

Tree of Love

(See Figure 494)

Maker: Unknown   **Name by:** Author
Colors made: Found only in white opalescent to date
Note: The name of this pattern is a variation of the *Tree of Life* name which graces far too many patterns at this time. I thought of calling it "Opalescent Tree of Life," but then some poor Portland Glass collector might see this advertised and think it is a rare piece of Portland pattern glass, which it most decidedly is not.

Tree Stump Mug

(See Figure 502)

Maker: Probably Northwood   **Name by:** Author
Colors made: green, white and blue opalescent

Tree Trunk Vase

(See Figure 440)

Maker: Northwood Glass, circa 1908
Name by: Har Op, pg. 108
Colors made: white, blue and green opalescent
Note: Sometimes signed with the Northwood trademark.

Twig (Vase)

(See Figure R)

Maker: Northwood Glass, circa 1910
Name by: Pres. 4, #74   **Other name:** Panelled Twig
Colors made: white, blue and canary opalescent; carnival
Note: Made in two sizes; beware of reproductions with the solid glass branches at the base.

Twig, Tiny

(See Figure 574)

Maker: Northwood Glass, circa 1910
Name by: Author
Colors made: white, blue, canary and rare in green opalescent; carnival

Twisted Ribs Vase

(See Figure 528)

Maker: Unknown   **Name by:** Author
Colors: The usual

Twister

(See Figure 478)

Maker: Unknown   **Name by:** Joe B. Bell
Colors: The usual

Vintage

(See Figure 445)
Maker: Jefferson Glass Co.'s #245 pattern, with later production in carnival colors by Northwood
Name by: Har Op, pg. 109
Colors made: white, blue and green opalescent; carnival glass; also in amethyst glass

Wheel & Block

(See Figure 505)
Maker: Northwood-Dugan glass, circa 1905
Name by: Har Op, pg. 111
Colors: white, blue and green opalescent; sometimes goofus decorated
Note: This pattern was previously attributed incorrectly to Jefferson. My attribution is based on the goofus pieces found in this pattern, as well as the 1905 Butler Brothers catalogue mentioned on page 11.

Windflower, Opalescent

(See Figure 521)
Maker: Uncertain   **Name:** Presnick 1, #208
Colors made: primarily carnival; rare in opalescent
Note: The word "opalescent" must precede the name of this pattern, to differentiate between this and the much earlier pattern listed by Kamm.

Winter Cabbage

(See Figure 406)
Maker: Northwood Glass, circa 1904   **Name by:** Author
Colors made: white, blue and green opalescent
Note: This is a variant of the *Cabbage Leaf* and I have named it as above due to the fewer number of leaves around the sides.

Winterlily

(See Figure 485)
Maker: Unknown   **Name by:** Author
Colors reported: Only white opalescent to date; others likely

Wishbone & Drapery

(See Figure 477)
Maker: Jefferson Glass Co., circa 1903   **Name by:** Author
Colors: white, blue and green opalescent
Note: See the Jefferson ad reprint in Book 1, page 53.

Woven Wonder

(See Figures 488 & 520)
Maker: Undoubtedly Northwood, circa 1908
Name by: Author
Colors: white and blue opalescent reported to date
Note: Attribution is based on the exact match of the weaving to the pattern found on "Rose Show" and "Frosted Leaf & Basketweave." Comparison reveals a similarity which is too much to be a coincidence.

Zippers & Loops

(See Figure 80)
Maker: Jefferson Glass Co., circa 1903.
Name by: Author   **Colors:** Green, blue and white opalescent
Note: The pattern appeared on a page of the Jefferson catalogue which I studied.

OUR "VENETIAN AND OPALESCENT" NOVELTY ASSORTMENT.

An incomparable group of 10 cent leaders.

C882—Big new fancy shape pieces in the rich opalescent and Venetian glass, most of which are actually worth double the price here named. Asst. comprises 12 articles, each one in asstd. colors such as blue, green, canary, amethyst, etc. ⅓ doz. each of the following:

9½ in. fancy footed opalescent salad dish.	Large nut or rose bowl on 3 fancy feet.
6 in. fancy shape Venetian vase.	9 in. fancy footed salad dish.
8¼ in. fancy footed comport or card tray.	6¾ in. twisted Venetian vase.
6½ in. fancy Venetian vase.	8½ in. diamond cut table dish.
8 in. deep flaring fruit bowl.	10 in. extra large opalescent vase.
Large size, fancy shape Venetian rose bowl	
8¾ in. tall ear of corn vase.	

80c
Per dozen,
Total 6 doz. in bbl., (Bbl. 35c.)

Grouping of Northwood-Dugan pieces: The above provided documentation that novelty patterns like **Palm & Scroll, Keyhole, Wheel & Block,** and **Reflecting Diamonds** came from the same factory as the well-known **Corn Vase.**

Grouping of Jefferson pieces: This provided the data necessary to attribute patterns like **Barbells, Astro, Popsickle Sticks** to the same company that made the popular **Tokyo** pattern.

OUR "BEST" OPALESCENT ASSORTMENT.

12 big new fancy pieces in the ever popular opalescent ware which can be retailed at a dime.

C871 — New shapes and new fancy designs, all pieces extra large, every one of them would retail readily at from 15 to 25c. Equally asstd. in the 3 best selling colors—blue, green and flint opalescent. Asst. comprises ½ doz. each of the following:

9 in. Large fancy footed salad bowl.	9 in. Footed fancy shape salad dish.
6⅝ " High footed salver.	5½ " High footed jelly dish.
6¼ " Extra deep high footed bowl.	8½ " Fancy table dish.
9 " Fancy footed fruit-dish.	8 " Deep high footed comport.
8½ " Large fancy round bread or cake plate.	12 " Tall fancy flower vase.
6½ " Extra deep fancy nut dish.	9 " Extra large footed salad dish.
Total 6 doz. in bbl. (Bbl. 35c.)	Per dozen, **79c**

Grouping of Jefferson pieces: This ad provided proof that patterns like **Beaded Fleur-de-Lis, Ruffles & Rings** and **Dahlia Twist** came from the same factory that produced **Beaded Fan (Shell & Dots)**.

OUR "GREATEST" OPALESCENT NOVELTY ASSORTMENT.
These magnificent 10c leaders are comparable only with 25c offerings of others.

C881 — Beautiful opalescent ware, equally asstd. in the three best selling colors, namely— blue, green and flint opalescent. Note especially the extra large size of the pieces. All shapes and designs are entirely new and very attractive. Asst. comprises ⅓ doz. each of 12 articles as follows:

9 in. fancy shape salad or berry dish with scalloped edge on 3 fancy feet.
8¼ in. extra large salad dish on 3 fancy feet
8½ in. high footed comport or fruit bowl.
6½ in. extra deep high footed nut bowl.
8¼ in. high footed fruit bowl, crimped edge.
9 in. footed card receiver, scalloped crimped edge.
6½ in. deep footed flaring nut bowl.

Tall flaring serpentine twisted vase, ht. 7 in.
6¼ in. extra deep bowl on 3 feet, crimped edge.
Large fancy footed rose bowl, ht. 5¼ in.
6½ in. high footed deep comport.
8¼ in. extra large footed scalloped edge dish.
Total, 6 doz. in bbl. (*Bbl. 35c*).

Per dozen, **80c**

FANCY OPALESCENT BASKET AND SALAD DISH ASST.
You can retail these at 25 cents although they will easily bring more.

C910 — Extra large fancy shaped pieces in beautiful full finished opalescent ware. Asst. comprises ¼ doz. each of 4 extra large pieces as follows:

9½ in. Extra Large Salad or Fruit Dish, genuine ruby color, crimped edge.

9 in. Extra Large and Deep Berry and Fruit Bowl on 4 feet, asstd. blue and green opalescent.

11 in. Extra Deep Footed Salad or Fruit Dish, fancy crimped and scalloped edge.

7¾ in. Extra Large and Deep Footed Basket with fancy rustic handle, asstd. blue and green opalescent.

Total, 2 doz. in bbl.
(*Bbl. 35c.*)   Per dozen, **$1.75**

Grouping of Jefferson pieces: Further proof that Jefferson made **Swag with Brackets** is shown here. The footed basket is the larger version of the **Old Man Winter** basket shown as Fig. 210, which has no feet. The blown ruffle-edge bowls are in the **Buttons & Braids** and **Coinspot** patterns.

English Opalescent Pressed Glass
(Illustrations Page 88)

I can state unequivocally that I know very little about the Victorian glass which was made in England, despite the fact that the entire era was named after their reigning queen. If it were not for the exceptionally fine publication by Geoffrey A. Godden, "Antique Glass and China," I wouldn't be able to report a single maker here.

With only one color plate of English opalescent offered by me, this can hardly be called an "in-depth study." I have included these pieces for two reasons. First, I wanted my readers to be able to tell from a glance whether a piece they found was American or English. The latter has a definite look to it which is unlike our native production. The other reason is that, as far as I can tell, no one has ever attempted to name these lovely pieces before, so I am initiating a few names here for collectors. This is nothing more than a start. A later sequel on opalescent glass will include many more patterns.

The English opalescent pressed glass era predates ours by a good ten years. There is little doubt that Northwood's English heritage, and even his well-known extended visit to England during the National Glass Company trauma, directly influenced much of the pressed opalescent production which enjoyed its hey-day after the turn of the century. Just take a look at the display of English pieces and then take a look at the signed Northwood tumbler in Figure 387, and you can see what I mean.

The primary producer of English opalescent was George Davidson & Co., of Gateshead-on-Tyne, England. Other opalescent production, on a smaller scale, was undertaken at Sowerby & Company, also at Gateshead, which had the distinction of being the largest pressed glass factory in the world at its peak, and finally Greener & Co. of Sunderland, England. I will not go into details on the history of these firms here, since I couldn't do it proper justice. But I **can** recommend Mr. Godden's wonderful publication.

Ascot

(See Figure 551)
Maker: Uncertain   **Y.O.P.:** circa 1890
Colors: Blue and canary opalescent

Chippendale

(See Figure 552)
Maker: George Davidson & Co.   **Y.O.P.:** circa 1885
Colors: blue and canary opalescent

Coronation

(See Figure 555)
Maker: Greener & Co., Sunderland   **Y.O.P.:** 1887
Colors: blue opalescent

Contessa

(See Figure 547)
Maker: Not certain   **Y.O.P.:** circa 1888
Colors: blue opalescent known

Crown Jewels

(See Figures 549-550)
Maker: Uncertain   **Y.O.P.:** circa 1888
Colors: blue opalescent

Piccadilly

(See Figure 548)
Maker: Sowerby & Co., Gateshead-on-Tyne
Y.O.P.: circa 1880
Colors known: green opalescent, opaque colors

Richelieu

(See Figures 556-557)
Maker: Davidson & Co.   **Y.O.P.:** circa 1885
Colors: blue and canary opalescent

War of Roses

(See Figures 554)
Maker: George Davidson & Co.   **Y.O.P.:** circa 1885
Colors: blue and canary opalescent

William & Mary

(See Figures 553, 565)
Maker: Unknown   **Y.O.P.:** circa 1885
Colors: canary opalescent

Fig. P
Daisy & Button
(bun tray)

Fig. Q
Diamond Maple Leaf
(Dugan Glass)

Illustrations of

Opalescent Novelties

(Includes Examples of English
Opalescent Glass)

Fig. T
*Strawberry and
Dahlia Twist*
(epergne)

Fig. R
panelled
Twig (Vase)
(rare/green)

Fig. S
Fish-in-the-Sea
(vase)

401
Ocean Shell

402
Beaded Fleur-de-Lis

403
Leaf Chalice

404
Beaded Star Medallion
(gas shade)

405
Sir Lancelot

406
Winter Cabbage

407
Cabbage Leaf

(basket)

408
Heart-Handled Open O's

409
Jefferson Wheel

410
Jackson

411
Reflecting Diamonds

412
Abalone

413
Ring-Handled Basket

414
Hearts & Clubs

415
Dolphin Compote

416
Dolphin &
Herons

417
Dolphin
Petticoat

415
Dolphin
Compote

417

418
Blossom & Palm

419
Daisy & Plume

420
Three Fruits

421
ree Fruits with Meander

422
Grapes & Cherries

423
Greek Key & Scales

424
Beaded Stars

425
Netted Roses

426
Bushel Basket

427
Heatherbloom

428
Little Nell

429
Zippers & Loops

430
Boggy Bayou

431
Palm & Scroll

432
Keyhole

433
Simple Simon

434
Everglades
(rare green)

435
Maple Leaf

436
Hilltop Vine

437
Jewel & Jan

438
Desert Garden

439
Daisy Dear

440
Tree Trunk

441
Cherry Panels

442
Heisey's
Pineapple & Fan

443
Overlapping Leaves

444
Reflections

445
Vintage

446
Piasa Bird

447
Palisades

448
Rose Show
(carnival opalescent)

449
Spool

450
Jewels & Drapery

451
Fan

452
ine-Cut & Roses

453
Poinsettia Lattice

454
Berry Patch

455
Waterlily
with Cattails

456 Pearl Flowers

457 Fluted Bars & Beads

458 Maple Leaf Chalice

459 Palisades

460 Hearts & Flowers

461 Cashews

462 Spokes & Wheels

463 Blocked Thumbprint & Beads

464 Scheherezade

465 Coinspot, Pressed

466 Basketweave Base, Open-Edged

467 Beaded Cable

468 Shell & Wild

469 Diamond Point & Fleur-de-Lis

470 Waterlily with Cattails

471 Lattice Medallions

472
Spool

473
*Aurora
Borealis*

474
*Miniature
Epergne*

475   476
Beads & Bark

477
Wishbone & Drape

478
Twister

479
Reverse Drapery

480
Fancy Fantails

481
Blackberry

482
Button Panels

483
Pearls & Scales

484
Cornucopia

485
Winterlily

486
Dragonlady

487
Laura

488
Woven Wonder
(rose bowl)

489
Blossoms & Web

490
Jolly Bear

491
Leaf & Leaflets

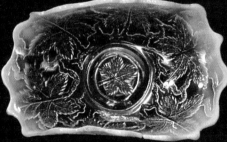

492
Autumn Leaves

493
Leaf & Diamonds

494
Tree of Love

495
Hobnail-in-Square

496
Thistle Patch

497
Grape & Cable
(punch bowl)

498
Milky Way

84

499
Corn Vase

500
Stork & Rushes
(mug)

501
Opal Open
(rose bowl)

502
Stump Mug

503
Grapevine Cluster

504
Leaf & Beads

505
Wheel & Block

506
Beads & Curly-Cues

507
Meander

508
Beaded Drapes

509
Jewel & Flower

510
Many Loops

511
Roulette

512
Ruffles & Rings

513
Tokyo

514
Northern Star
(chop plate)

515
Beaded Jan
(rose bowl)

516
Coral

517
Barbells

518
Astro

519
Carousel

520
Woven Wonder

521
Windflower

522
Popsickle Sticks

523
Sea Spray
(olive)

524
Open O's

525
Spool &
Threads

526
Blooms & Blossoms
(olive)

527
Diamond
Point

528
Twisted
Ribs

529
Feathers

530
Piasa Bird

531
Fish-in-
the-Sea

532
Diamond
& Oval
Thumbprint

533
Jewels &
Drapery

534
Calyx

535
Fluted Scrolls
with Vine

536
Lined
Heart

537
Lorna

538
Diamond
Stem

539
Concave
Columns

540
Many
Ribs

541
Jefferson's
Spool

542
Beads
& Bark

543
Dahlia
Twist

544
Aurora
Borealis

545
Fluted Bars
and Beads

546
Corn Vase

English Opalescent

547
Coronation

548
Piccadilly

549

550
Crown Jewels

551
Ascot

552
Contessa

553
William & Mary

554
War of Roses

555
Chippendale

556

Richelieu

557

REPRODUCTION OPALESCENT GLASS
(includes items of *questionable* age)

See illustrations pgs. 95-96

Westmoreland Reproductions made in green opalescent only
(also reproduced in water set, cruet)

Here we go again! Reproductions — the thorn in every dealer and collector's foot. Not just glassware is being reproduced, but china, furniture, pewter, bisque, metal, paintings, virtually anything of value. My position on reproductions is well-known, and I can only hope that enough pressure can be initiated by collectors to urge passage of legislation requiring permanent marking of any type of reproduction. Wouldn't the 1976 Bicentennial have been perfect timing for passage of such a bill?

I simply cannot understand how a handful of money-grubbing opportunists can be permitted to fraud the public with reproductions being placed on the market, whereas virtually every other form of fraud is considered a punishable crime. For my part, I continue to write my Congressman urging action on any bill making reproductions illegal unless marked as such. I only hope that you will do the same.

Regarding the reproductions in my field, colored pattern glass, there are enough to frighten away any beginner collector from ever investing a dime. Their untrained eye cannot tell the difference. Even the advanced collectors and enthusiasts like myself can sometimes be fooled. I am still having a terrible time deciding by whom and when the "Inverted Fan & Feather" rose bowls were made. I have included them with the reproductions until a definite report can be made. I would rather have it shown here than with legitimate antiques, because if I am right about their questionable age, then no one will be hurt. But if I had listed them elsewhere, then learned that they were reproductions later, hundreds of investors would have been misguided into buying them.

My own knowledge about reproductions is considerably limited. I can pretty well tell whether a piece of glass is old or not, but I cannot date the reproduction, and in most cases cannot tell you who made it. Some of the blown patterns were reproduced in the thirties (I am told), and I wasn't even born then. No enterprising author appears to have kept track of this new glass back then (like many publications do today) and documented it for posterity.

Despite this drawback, a number of known reproductions in opalescent glass are illustrated on pages 95 & 96. These were made from around 1940 to the present day production undertaken by Westmoreland and L. G. Wright.

Not all recent opalescent production can be termed reproductions. Companies like Duncan & Miller produced entire new lines of opalescent wares, but these items were designed with modern tastes in mind, and they should fool no one into thinking they were Victorian.

A word of thanks to Lynn Welker for loaning me many of the pieces of reproduction glass shown here and for also preparing the information regarding them. It is of interest, I am sure, that several of the reproductions were loaned from collectors who were "fooled." I prefer to use the word "defrauded" in this case.

Argonaut Shell

(Fig. 625)
Company: L. G. Wright　　　**Y.O.P.:** 1970-1971
Colors made: blue
Pieces made: tumbler, toothpick, salt and pepper, jelly compote, butter, creamer, sugar, large and small berry bowls
Notes: Opalescence tends to be very poor, only a small top edge being opalescent.

Baby Coinspot

(Fig. 620)
Company: Fenton
Y.O.P.: 1950's, very short production
Colors made: cranberry, possibly blue
Pieces made: sugar shaker, creamer, butterdish (has clear twig finial and milk glass base), rosebowl, vases
Notes: Fenton renamed this pattern, Polka Dot. Beware of reeded handles.

Beatty Honeycomb

(Fig. 591, 597, 618)
Company: Fenton
Y.O.P.: 1960—for a very short time
Colors made: blue, dark green
Pieces made: covered sugar, rosebowl, basket, vase
Notes: Old Beatty honeycomb was never made in this shade of green.

Blown Twist

(Fig. 603)
Company: Fenton
Y.O.P.: Early 1950's—very limited prod.
Colors made: Blue, cranberry, white, usually with a satin finish
Pieces made: Fairy lamp, vases, rosebowl
Notes: These pieces are often attributed to Nailsea but are heavier than the old ones.

Bubble Lattice

(Fig. 614)
Company: Fenton
Y.O.P.: mid-1950's, very short production
Colors made: blue, cranberry, dark green
Pieces made: rosebowl, vases, lamps
Notes: Never made in old in the green opalescent. The new pieces also lack the ribbing of the old.

Cactus

(Fig. 602)
Company: Fenton
Y.O.P.: 1959-1960
Colors made: Yellow
Pieces made: salt and pepper, cruet, tri-corner nappy, jelly compote, bowls, sugar, creamer, long stick butter, candlesticks, basket, cakestand, vases
Notes: No cactus was made in old opalescent

Coinspot

(Opal dots)
(Not pictured)
Company: Fenton for L. G. Wright
Y.O.P.: long production, late 1940's-present
Colors made: blue, cranberry
Pieces made: water pitcher, tumbler, creamer, cruet, sugar shaker, pickle castor, lamps including the miniature
Notes: L. G. Wright renamed this pattern, Opalescent Dot. Beware of reeded handles.

Corn Vase

(Fig. 613)
Company: L. G. Wright
Y.O.P.: possibly 1950's-1960's
Colors made: blue and yellow
Pieces made: vase only
Notes: Top of the new vase does not extend into long points as the old one does.

Daisy & Button

(Fig. 596)
Company: Fenton (also made for L. G. Wright and A. & A. Importing)
Y.O.P.: mid-1950's-present
Colors made: blue, yellow, white
Pieces made: virtually every table piece as well as novelties such as hats, shoes, match holders, etc.
Notes: Daisy and button not known in any old pieces at the present.

Daisy & Fern

(Fig. 606, 611)
Company: Fenton for L. G. Wright
Y.O.P.: long production (late 1940's-present)
Colors made: blue, yellow cranberry
Pieces made: water pitcher, tumbler, milk pitcher, 2 sizes of covered jars, barber bottle, syrup, creamer, cruet, sugar shaker, pickle castor, full-sized lamps
Notes: Beware of reeded handles.

Dolphin Candlesticks

(Fig. 590)
Company: Westmoreland for A. & A. Importing
Y.O.P.: 1973-1975
Colors made: dark blue
Pieces made: candlesticks only

Dolphin Stem

(Fig. 600)
Company: Westmoreland for L. G. Wright
Y.O.P.: possibly early 1950's into 1960's, fairly long but not continuous production

Colors made: blue, yellow, white
Pieces made: compote, candlesticks

Flattened Diamond & Sunburst

(Fig. 629)
Company: Westmoreland
Y.O.P.: 1975
Colors made: dark blue and dark green
Pieces made: child's punch bowl and cups
Notes: This was never made in old opalescent glass.

Hand Vase

(Fig. 627)
Company: Unknown
Y.O.P.: 1960's
Colors made: blue, yellow, white
Pieces made: Several sizes of vases.

Hobnail

(Fig. 621, 622, 626)
Company: Fenton (also for A. & A. Importing and various lamp companies)
Imperial Glass Co.
Possibly a foreign glass company
Y.O.P.: 1930's-present
Colors made: pale and deep blue, yellow, cranberry, white, dark green, and dark purple (the same color as the old purple opalescent water-lily and cattail pieces)
Pieces made: Virtually all table pieces as well as many different novelties
Notes: The only reproduction in the Hobbs' type hobnail is a foreign cruet seen in an ugly yellow opalescent and the covered butter in blue and yellow opal. Don't be afraid to buy the Hobbs' type hobnail. However, beware of the pressed-type hobnails as they have been so heavily reproduced for so long. In 1965-1967, Imperial made a large line of pressed hobnail in yellow including fan-edged berry bowls in large and small sizes. Beware of reeded handles

Inverted Fan & Feather

(Fig. 612)
Company: Unknown
Y.O.P.: unknown but very probably in the late 1930's or early 1940's as many of these pieces have been in collections for a long time
Colors made: blue, yellow, white
Pieces made: Rosebowl, flat card tray or plate on feet
Notes: Never seen with gold decor like the old.

Jersey Swirl

(Fig. 599)
Company: L. G. Wright
Y.O.P.: 1968-1970
Colors made: yellow
Pieces made: goblet, wine
Notes: No old Jersey Swirl was made in opalescent glass.

Moon & Star

(Fig. 617, 594)
Company: L. G. Wright
Y.O.P.: mid-1950's-1965, 1968-1970
Colors made: yellow
Pieces made: goblet, wine, lamps including the miniature, possibly other pieces
Notes: No old moon and star was made in opalescent glass.

Orange Tree

(Fig. 601)
Company: Fenton for A. & A. Importing
Y.O.P.: 1973
Colors made: blue, yellow
Pieces made: rosebowl only
Notes: This rosebowl was not originally made in opalescent glass.

Panelled Grape

(Fig. 609-610)
Company: Westmoreland for L. G. Wright
Y.O.P.: 1950's (blue), 1968-1970 (yellow)
Colors made: blue, yellow
Pieces made: water pitcher, tumblers in several sizes, goblet, wine, covered compote, probably other pieces
Notes: Old panelled grape was not made in opalescent glass.

Peacock

(Fig. 615, 617)
Company: Westmoreland for A. & A. Importing
Y.O.P.: 1973-1975
Colors made: dark blue
Pieces made: covered sugar and covered cream
Notes: This pattern of sugar and creamer not made in old opalescent glass.

Polka Dot

(Fig. 595)
Company: Fenton for L. G. Wright
Y.O.P.: long production, late 1940's-1970
Colors made: blue, cranberry, yellow
Pieces made: barber bottle, tumbler, lamps, cruet, creamer
Notes: L. G. Wright renamed this pattern, Opalescent Eye Dot. Beware of reeded handles.

Polka Dot

(Fig. 607, 619, 628)
Company: Fenton (also for lamp companies)
Y.O.P.: long production although not continuous since the 1940's
Colors made: pale and medium blue, cranberry, yellow, white, deep green
Pieces made: water pitcher, tumbler, cruet, barber bottle, rosebowl, hats, many different shapes and sizes of vases, lamps
Notes: Fenton called this Coinspot. No true counterpart in old opalescent glass. Beware of reeded handles.

Stars & Stripes

(Fig. 623)
Company: Fenton for L. G. Wright
Y.O.P.: long production although not continuous
Colors made: blue, cranberry
Pieces made: tumbler, creamer, barber bottle, cruet (from 1940's)
Notes: The new is almost as hard to find as the old. Beware of reeded handles.

Stripe

(Fig. 624)
Company: Fenton (also for L. G. Wright)
Y.O.P.: long production, late 1940's-present
Colors made: blue, yellow, cranberry, white, pale green and dark green
Pieces made: barber bottle for L. G. Wright, salt and pepper, wine bottle, vases, many different lamps
Notes: L. G. Wright renamed this line Opal. Rib. Fenton also made this in a white opalescent line in 1959. The shapes are very modern and would not be confused with the old. Beware of reeded handles.

Swirl, Opal

(Fig. 604, 605)
Company: Fenton (also made for L. G. Wright and various lamp companies)
Y.O.P.: long production, late-1940's-present
Colors made: blue, cranberry, yellow
Pieces made: water pitcher, tumbler, milk pitcher, barber bottle, syrup, creamer, cruet, sugar shaker, pickle castor, hats, lamps including the miniature
Notes: Fenton renamed this Spiral. Beware of reeded handles.

Thumbprint

(Fig. 598)
Company: Fenton
Y.O.P.: 1960's-short production
Colors made: yellow
Pieces made: basket, possibly other pieces
Notes: The old pressed thumbprint pattern was never made in opalescent glass.

Town Pump & Trough

(Not pictured)
Company: L. G. Wright
Y.O.P.: 1950's
Colors made: blue, yellow
Pieces made: pump, trough
Notes: The top of the pump is flat and does not have the fancy irregular top of the old one, neither piece is signed.

Vesta

(Fig. 592, 593)
Company: Fenton (also for A. & A. Importing)
Y.O.P.: 1950's-short production, again in 1973-1973 for A. & A.
Colors made: blue, white, possibly yellow
Pieces made: Vases, two sizes of epergnes

Windows

(Fig. 608)
Company: Fenton for L. G. Wright
Y.O.P.: long production, 1950's-present
Colors made: blue, cranberry
Pieces made: water pitcher, tumbler, milk pitcher, syrup, creamer, cruet, lamps including the miniature
Notes: L. G. Wright renamed this pattern, Honeycomb. Beware of reeded handles.

Wreathed Cherry

(Not pictured)
Company: L. G. Wright
Y.O.P.: 1968-1970
Colors made: yellow
Pieces made: creamer, ruffled top, open sugar, possibly other pieces

Assorted Tiny Things

(toothpick holders, salt dips, etc . . .)

558 **Idyll**

559 **Wreath & Shell** (salt dip)

560 **Beatty Honeycomb**

561 **Beatty Rib**

562 **Twist** (mini. spooner)

Panelled Sprig

564 **Shell**

565 **William & Mary** (master salt—English)

566 **Polka Dot**

567 **Over-All Ho**

568   569 **Gonterman Swirl**

570 **Fern**

571 **Ring-Handle Basket**

572 **Reverse Swirl** (ring neck)

573 **Beaded Ovals in Sand** (nappy)

574 **Tiny Twig** (vase)

(The above are *not* reproductions)

Assorted Tiny Things

575
Spanish Lace
(mini. bride's bowl)

576
Colonial Stairsteps
(toothpick)

577
Jackson
(mini. epergne)

578
Bullseye
(gas shade)

579
Seaweed

580
Opal. Swirl

581
Circled Scroll

582 583
Beatty Honeycomb
(salts)

584
Diamond Spearhead
(mug)

585 586
Beatty Ribbed Opal
(match)   (toothpick)

587
(mustard)

588
Beatty Honeycomb
(mug)

589
(indiv. creamer)

(The above are *not* reproductions)

Reproduction Opalescent Glass (a representative example)

590

591

592

593

594

595

596

597

598

599

600

601

602

603

604

605

606

607

608

Reproduction Opalescent Glass   (a representative example)

609

610

611

612 *Not A Reproduction*

613

614

615

616

617

618

619

620

621

622

623

624

625

626

627

628

629

VI

Early Ad & Catalogue Reprints

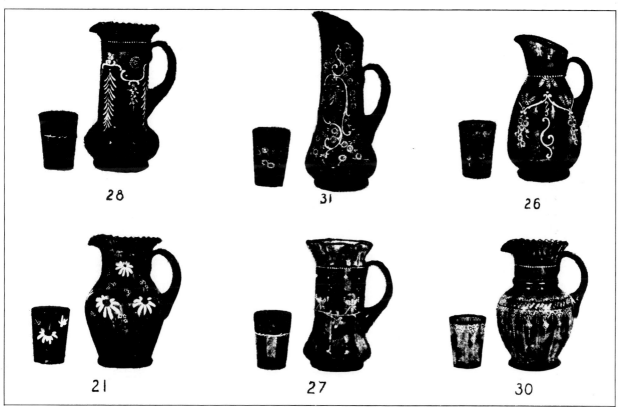

LEMONADE SETS. BY H. NORTHWOOD & CO.

28   31   26

21   27   30

The shapes characteristic of Northwood Production.

......Order here.

Our "MOORISH QUEEN" OPALESCENT WATER SET.

The Richest and Most Eloquent Of all our Self-Talking Attractions.

As a "DOLLAR LEADER" it is Given Away!

Words can but mar the rare, indescribable beauty of this gorgeous table outfit. We can simply explain that the set comprises: 1 large one-half gallon pitcher, 1 large silverine tray, 2 tumblers and 1 slop bowl—all to match. Put up 2 sets of each color,—Ruby, Blue, Canary and Crystal Opalescent,—making a total of 8 sets to bbl. (Sold only by bbl.)   **Price, 62c per Set.**

"Bubble Lattice"

Our "Palace Art Lamp."
Superbly Rich, Yet Practically Useful.

This truly artistic lamp has a satin art glass vase body 8½ in. in diameter, with real bronze, 8 inch base; it stands complete, 21½ in. high. It has a separate oil fount of spun brass set into a brass lined compartment in an absolutely safe manner; satin art dome and 10-inch shade to match; bronze globe holder, chimney and wick complete; a "duplex" double wick burner with gold bronze finish, nicely fitted with a cord and tassel extinguisher. Put up 2 colors in case, one rich rose red and the other a soft turquoise blue, making a total of two complete lamps in case. Sold only by case.

....Order here.   **Price, $3.25 each.**

"Reverse Swirl"

Our "Oriental Harem" Or Soft Twilight Lamp.

Now a 50-Cent Article for the First Time.

This is the most elegant of all "color effect" lamps. The body is of genuine Venetian ribbed opalescent glass, standing on a solid brass 4½-inch base. It has a dome shade (supported by brass holding arms) in color to match the body of the lamp. Assorted one of each color, rose, turquoise, canary and pearl opalescent, making a total of ⅓ doz. in a box. No charge for box.   **Price, $3.45 Doz.**

....Order here.

"Reverse Swirl"

Our "Brass Base" NIGHT LAMP.

A 25-Cent Gem.

The glass portion of this exquisite little lamp comes in assorted shades, viz: rose, turquoise, canary and crystal opalescent. Nicely put up ½ doz. in box, including burners, chimneys and wicks.   **Price, $2.10 Doz.**

.....Order here.

"Reverse Swirl"

Our "Venetian Beauty" GLOBE NIGHT LAMP.

"A 25-Cent Opalescent Beauty."

The newest of shapes; wide globe chimney; all made in the new ribbed opalescent glass. Each lamp complete with wick, burner and chimney. Put up ½ dozen in box.   **Price, $1.90 Doz.**

...Order here.

"Venetian Globe" CHIMNEYS.

Customers wishing extra chimneys for the above lamp can be supplied. 1 doz. in box.
..... Order here,   **84c Doz.**

Pattern?

Our "TUSCAN" TOOTH-PICK.
Another World Beater for 10 cents.

This is an exquisite little pick holder, made in this beautiful and delicate striped ware. Three different shades (ruby, blue and crystal opalescent) in each dozen. An article that only needs to be shown to create a "buying fever." 1 doz. in box.
..... Order here   **Price, 78c Doz.**

"Opal Swirl"

OUR "SATIN OPALESCENT" TOOTH-PICK.
A Gem of Art for 10 Cents.

The handsomest thing you ever saw for the price. Assorted in equal quantities, ruby, blue, canary and crystal opalescent, with ground bottoms. 1 dozen in box.
........Order here.   **Price, 83c Doz.**

"Reverse Swirl"

OUR "SATIN GRECIAN" SALT.
An Exquisite 10-Cent Beauty.

This salt shaker has proven one of the most phenomenal sellers since the day it first appeared. The blending of colors here represented is unprecedented. Assorted in ruby, blue, canary and crystal opalescent tints; and all having best nickel caps. 1 doz. in box.
......Order here.   **Price, 82c Doz.**

OUR "SATIN GRECIAN" PEPPER.
Same as the above, but with small perforations.
........Order here.   **Price 82c Doz.**

"Bubble Lattice"

Our New "VENETIAN CASTER."
Remodeled so as not to Break.

An Exquisite $1.00 Offering.

The bottles are of the beautiful Venetian glass assorted in four colors of ruby, turquoise, crystal and canary. It has a genuine nickel frame and handle. Superior to any silver-plated caster. Each caster has 4 bottles—vinegar, pepper, mustard and salt. Each caster in a handsome wood box. Sold in any quantity, and no charge for package.
.....Order here.   **Price, 63c Each**

"Opal Stripe"

"VENETIAN" SUGAR SHAKER.
A Dining Table Beauty TO SELL FOR A "QUARTER."

The prize of all prizes. This is without exception the handsomest thing offered by us this season. Every table needs a sugar sifter and this one at 25 cents will prove a marvelous seller. ½ doz. in box
......Order here   **$2.00 Doz.**

"Reverse Swirl"

THE JEFFERSON GLASS CO. Steubenville, Ohio

Early Jefferson Glass ad (circa 1904) which shows the shape of their water pitchers.

NOT SOLD THROUGH IRRESPONSIBLE AGENTS.

No. 11.

Lemonade Set.

Crystal Opalescent,
Blue Opalescent,
Rose Opalescent,
Or Plain Ruby.

If you have not ordered your

Lemonade Sets

Better do it NOW.

Prices never so low.
Quality and Style
Unexcelled—over 50
Styles in our variety,
Running from
$3.75 to $18.00 per doz.

This ad appeared in 1902, and was undoubtedly a set produced by Beaumont Glass Co., Martins Ferry, O.

IRIS

PLAIN ● COLORED ● OPALESCENT

The Jefferson Glass Co.

Geo. Mortimer, *Dice-Pres.*
G. Grant Fish, *Treas. & Gen'l Mgr.*   **Steubenville, Ohio**

See our display Pittsburg, Pa., Monongahela House, Geo. Mortimer

3

An assortment of "Iris with Meander" glass (originally called "Iris")

VII

CORRECTIONS AND ADDITIONS TO BOOK I

(FIRST EDITION ONLY)

PATTERN	NOTE	PAGE
ARCHED OVALS	Proven to be U.S. Glass pattern now.	14
BEAD AND SCROLL	Also made in cobalt blue (rare)	14
BEADED SWIRL & DISC	Also made by U.S. Glass Co., circa 1900; I have seen an old catalogue from this firm since publication	15
BEATTY HONEYCOMB	No green opalescent was ever made originally; these turned out to be reproductions (see page 618)	15
BLOCKED THUMBPRINT	Should be referred to as "Blocked Thumbprint Band"	15
BOHEMIAN	Also made in a frosted camphor-type glass with color-stained flowers	16
BRITTANIC	Rare in emerald green	17
COLORADO	Also made in yellow-green, circa 1920	19
CROESUS	IS NOW BEING REPRODUCED IN A TUMBLER AND **ALL FOUR** PIECES TO THE TABLE SET! New toothpicks also in crystal.	21
DOYLE'S HONEYCOMB	This is the miniature spooner to the child's table set. Also made in blue, amber and rare in amethyst.	22
FANCY LOOP	The toothpick has been found with a marigold flashing, identical in color to Figure 167 Leaf & Star toothpick.	24
FRAZIER	It can now be confirmed that this was indeed a pattern made by U.S. Glass. I was given an opportunity to study one of their old catalogues.	26
HOBNAIL, FRANCES WARE	It has now been learned that the toothpick illustrated as Fig. 143 also served as a toy tumbler to a child's water set. A reader sent me this data, and a copy of an old Hobbs catalogue to substantiate.	28
JEWELLED HEART	The toothpick was also made in blue, but not with opalescence.	28
KITTENS	Made by Fenton, circa 1910	29
LEAF MOLD	Also made in yellow-green satin	29
LEAF UMBRELLA	Also made in yellow satin	32
STRIPE, OPALES.	Also made in blue and canary opales.	34
OPTIC, PRESSED	Kamm called this "Inside Ribbing," so **it was** previously listed (but not attributed)	37
RIBBED DRAPE	Also made in apple green	39
ROYAL OAK	Very very rare in amber-stained glass	39
RUBY THUMBPRINT	Rare in amber-stained glass	40
SHOESHONE	Also made in amber-stained glass	41
SPEARPOINT BAND	The "Gothic" pattern made by McKee	41
SPRIG, PANELLED	This may be Northwood, too. I have found an ad with this pattern, dated 1905 (Hobbs & Beaumont were closed then)	41
SUNK HONEYCOMB	This was made by McKee, and originally called their "Corona" pattern.	42
SWIRL & LEAF	Reported in an unusual grey opaque	44
WILD ROSE WITH SCROLLING	This pattern was also made by McKee, circa 1915, in the toy set	45
X-RAY	This was not made in ruby or amber-stained. I misread the Beaumont ad.	46
PENNSYLVANIA	I recently learned that the straight-sided piece that most people refer to as a shot glass was offered in a 1905 Butler Bros. catalogue as the "tumbler-toothpick."	47
D & M #42	This pattern was definitely made in a full-size table service.	49
SUNBONNET BABIES	The existence of original "Baking Scene" pieces has not been confirmed to date	49
SNAKE ON A STUMP	This has not been reproduced, as it was reported in Boultinghouse	49

PATTERN INDEX

All patterns included in this volume are listed below in alphabetical order, followed by the page where pattern data can be found (in **boldface** type), followed then by page numbers where illustrations are located.